LENS ON OUTDOOR LEARNING

LENS ON OUTDOOR LEARNING

Wendy Banning & Ginny Sullivan

Redleaf Press®
www.redleafpress.org
800-423-8309

Published by Redleaf Press
10 Yorkton Court
St. Paul, MN 55117
www.redleafpress.org

First edition 2011
Cover design by Jim Handrigan
Interior typeset in Berkeley Oldstyle Book and designed by Erin Kirk New
Cover photo taken by Wendy Banning
Interior photos taken by Wendy Banning and Ginny Sullivan

Printed in the United States of America
17   16   15   14   13   12   11   10   1   2   3   4   5   6   7   8

Library of Congress Cataloging-in-Publication Data

Banning, Wendy.
    Lens on outdoor learning / Wendy Banning and Ginny Sullivan.—1st ed.
        p. cm.
      Includes bibliographical references.
      ISBN 978-1-60554-024-5 (alk. paper)
      1. Outdoor education. 2. Outdoor recreation for children. 3. Play environments.
4. Adventure education.   I. Sullivan, Ginny. II. Title.
      LB1047.B27 2010
      371.3'84—dc22
                                          2010017243

Printed on 10 percent postconsumer waste paper

For my dad, who shared nature's secrets with me and for whom each new bud, each hidden nest, each soaring bird, and all wild places were an endless source of wonder. And for my mother, who let me wander, explore, climb, get muddy, and have secret places; the childhood every child deserves.

W. B. B.

For my children—Phineas and Carrie and Katharine and Theo—and for their children—and the magical capacity within all children to take us back to the deep learning ground of sand, water, woods, and ponds.

V. M. S.

CONTENTS

Acknowledgments

THE RESEARCH AND FIELDWORK represented in this book were efforts of pure joy. The text reflects the generosity and creativity of many educators who opened their doors to us so that we could document the extraordinary exploration and learning that children experience each day in the outdoors. We especially thank Deborah Pollard at Orchard Hill and Donna King and Sarah Meyer at Children First for their generous support of the project and for the many hours they allowed us to spend observing and documenting learning in their environments. We are also grateful to Katie Mann of the More at Four program at Middle Fork Elementary School who welcomed our presence on her school yard in the early stages of her teaching outdoors as the project evolved in our minds. We thank Janet McGinnis, who has been enormously supportive of this project while devoting thousands of hours to educating caregivers and teachers in North Carolina and establishing, with Jani Kozlowski, the North Carolina Outdoor Learning Environments Alliance. We thank our colleagues in this group who have demonstrated the impressive benefits to children that result from a statewide structure where all stakeholders come to the table and learn from each other.

Wendy would like to thank the school principals who, during her years as a young teacher, supported and allowed her to be different. In particular, she thanks Sally Bragg, who let her take her class of young children (and their wheelchairs) camping in the mountains and adventuring at the coast so they could watch the stars overhead, hear waterfalls, and feel the early morning dew. She would also like to thank Belinda Locke who dared to dream with her about starting a school where children's connection to nature, learning, and one another could be sustained. She thanks Tandy Jones and Alison Hill who made the dream of creating a school possible by providing a beautiful site tucked in the woods of Chatham County, North Carolina. Most especially, Wendy thanks the teachers drawn to the school's holistic vision of education who worked to help make it a reality, including Ben Waugh, Gwen Overturf, Amy Guskiewicz, Walt Tysinger, Kate Peele, Candace Waken, Charlie Butchart, Sara Daily, and Sarah Carrington. Thanks, too, to Livy Ludington and Tori Ralston, her steadfast partners in creating Irvin Learning Farm.

Ginny would like to thank Barbara Fisher, who made it possible for her to spend her first years as a young teacher in the Early Childhood Unit of University Elementary School at UCLA, where the gully, the stream, and the sun-struck redwoods were a part of children's everyday experience. There, Dee Hanson and Madelyn Hunter provided an invaluable lens on learning, insisting always that she look closely at the details of what each child was actually doing and saying. Benjamin Barnes introduced her to the Plowden Report and the British Infant School and encouraged her to set no limits on the world children would engage with in her classrooms. She thanks Robin Moore for his seminal work elucidating children's connections to their places, which has inspired a growing body of empirical research establishing the benefits to children of time spent in nature. And lastly, she thanks Ruth Parnall, who has done more than her share of the work of Learning by the Yard while her coprincipal toiled on this manuscript.

We are grateful to our editors at Redleaf Press, Kyra Ostendorf and David Heath, for their immediate and enthusiastic response and endorsement of our project. From our first conversations with Redleaf, they made it clear that they understood and supported our project and were eager to make this book beautiful and accessible to caregivers, educators, and early childhood professionals.

Lastly we honor the partnership that the two of us, as coauthors, have shared. The past two years have been a journey in friendship, professional growth, and mutual discovery that has enriched both our lives.

LENS ON OUTDOOR LEARNING

Introduction

WE CAME TO THE PROCESS of writing this book with a strong conviction that the outdoors is unique in how it engages young children with learning. This conviction has its roots in the work we have done over many years and in many settings. Our own teaching experience, as well as our work designing both indoor and outdoor learning environments, training teachers, developing curriculum, and documenting children's growth and learning, have all shaped this certainty. Children behave differently outside. The outdoors offers opportunities for open-ended play and discovery that are not available indoors. Children's outdoor learning is deep and complex.

Many of the skills that teachers set out to teach formally and help children develop occur naturally in the outdoor environment. The outdoors is a space in which children's work and play spontaneously calls upon a broad range of cognitive aptitudes, including measurement, planning, problem-solving, and sequencing skills. It is also a space in which collaboration, communication, sharing, conflict resolution, and other important social skills are required and practiced. The natural world is fertile ground for the imagination. It inspires creativity and innovative projects that integrate the cognitive and creative aspects of children's thinking. The outdoors is, of course, also a rich and essential component for children's healthy physical development. It allows them to challenge themselves physically, supporting development of coordination, strength, motor planning, and physical competence. It challenges children to experiment, develop judgment, increase muscle strength, and build a deeper understanding and joyfulness around how their own bodies work.

In the less constrained setting of the outdoors, children feel freer to experiment, and try new things. Because it is open-ended and children's behavior within it is less prescribed, the outdoors supports valuable risk taking (Gill 2007). Children are more likely to stretch themselves and take cognitive, physical, and social-emotional risks. The opportunity to take these risks makes the outdoors a particularly fertile space for children's learning. They can test out theories, refine understandings, develop new skills, and grow in their sense of self as they experience their interconnectedness with the natural world and with one another.

A key component of children's learning involves them developing strategies around how they learn. To be effective learners, they must know how best to approach a task, break it down into manageable pieces, and anticipate what is coming next. They need occasions to develop resilience in the face of perceived failure and opportunities for inventiveness as they come up with new ways to approach a problem. Each of these learning aptitudes or approaches to learning naturally evolves and is strengthened within the content of children's experiences in the outdoors. All of these strategies learned and practiced outdoors are transferable and applicable to all learning and to all environments. They are equally effective in indoor classrooms, home environments, and the community.

An understanding and appreciation of the importance of outdoor learning is growing rapidly throughout the world. Outdoor learning is more and more the subject of research, early childhood conferences, courses, and professional publications. State quality rating and improvement systems and accreditation agencies increasingly look at the outdoor environment when they evaluate programs for excellence.

This focus on the outdoors challenges teachers to evaluate, rethink, and perhaps restructure their programs. Along with having to meet growing expectations around outdoor learning, teachers are also expected to engage with early learning standards, explicitly document and measure children's growth, and, in some programs, deliver increasingly formalized curricula. Many teachers feel the emphasis on spending more time outside is persuasive and exciting. However, they are concerned about their ability to satisfy the mounting expectations. It is hard to meet rigorous programmatic objectives set by early childhood organizations, licensing and regulatory agencies, and evaluators, as well as provide additional time outside. The demands are very real and restructuring programs to create more outdoor time is challenging.

Yet, in our study of children's outdoor learning experiences, the natural world emerges clearly as the educator's ally in confronting these multiple demands. The natural world is an unparalleled resource for children and teachers in meeting developmental and early learning goals. In our observations of children with unstructured time in the natural world, we consistently see them spontaneously engage with all of the attitudes and behaviors delineated in early learning standards across the country. This propitious alignment will be welcome news to teachers. Rather than detracting from time needed to pursue specific learning objectives, going outside enhances and supports all aspects of the expectations you have for children's learning, growth, and development. By creating well-planned outdoor learning spaces for children and including ample open-ended daily time within that outdoor environment, teachers support children's learning across all domains.

When we realized how perfectly children's behaviors and attitudes outdoors align with early learning standards, we knew we had the key teachers need to unlock the potential of the outdoors. We came to this realization by observing children closely and analyzing what they are really doing when they work and play outside. Having seen it ourselves, we wanted to share this insight with other teachers. To do this, we collected photographs and children's own words to tell the story of their learning in rich outdoor environments. This learning often occurs without being taught and without the direct intervention of an adult. As we analyzed the data we collected, we saw strong evidence of children meeting standards from all domains.

We were persuaded to focus initially on the approaches to learning domain because we see this domain as critical to children's future success in school. The approaches to learning domain is primarily about process, and addresses directly how children learn how to learn. It is also the domain that teachers tell us is the hardest to measure and the most challenging to plan for. How does one plan for curiosity, initiative, persistence, risk taking, and resilience? You will see in this book how the natural world answers this question by offering children opportunities to practice and develop these predispositions. The stories here show clearly how this works. They also portray the complex role of the educator in such settings. Children's play and learning are intertwined in these pages with descriptions of the educator's role.

Rich outdoor learning requires that one engage deeply with both the child and the environment. Much of the most effective "teaching" outdoors is indirect and involves provisioning, observing, and talking with children. You may see yourself in these stories, observing, noticing, adding a new tool to a work space, reading just the right book at story time to spark a new idea about the garden, or offering a question to help clarify the direction an investigation will take. It is our goal that you will emerge from reading this book with a new appreciation of the deep partnership that exists between you, the children you work with, and the environment outdoors in which your work together unfolds.

Too often teacher training equips teachers with the skills to provide quality indoor experiences for children but fails to help them develop the ability to observe, evaluate, and plan for children's learning outdoors. This book provides the guidance you need to do this. It provides a framework for integrating this important venue, the outdoors, more consciously into your teaching practice and incorporating it into your thinking and planning for children. Teachers who are trained to be careful observers of children's work and play outside and who understand the complexity of what children are doing are better equipped to support children's learning. Such teachers can suggest meaningful extensions or pose just the right question to stretch a child's thinking. They are able to think of new materials and opportunities that build upon the natural inclinations, interests, and questions evident in children's activities and choices.

The illustrated narratives at the heart of this book show what quality outdoor learning looks like in action. We collected these narratives in the field over a period of several years as we observed children at work and play. Often the narratives are rich with children's language as they make discoveries and communicate what they are seeing and feeling. At other times, the dialogue may be internal or between the child and the material so there are no words to quote. In the stories in which children are not speaking out loud, children's expressions, behaviors, and gestures tell a rich story. You will see how eloquent children are both with and without words.

The narratives that follow enable you to witness firsthand, through pictures, descriptions, and children's own words, the richness and complexity of children's learning outside. Each story invites you to use your imagination to enter the world of the child engaged with a project or a problem in an outdoor setting. Each story is followed by a discussion of the particular role the outdoors plays in the unfolding of the narrative. For example, how does the outdoors uniquely contribute to the activity that is described? How is the role of the teacher instrumental in the child's experience? Finally, each story and its significance is analyzed to reveal the important learning taking place.

In addition to elucidating children's learning, the book examines in detail the complementary roles of the child, the environment, and the educator as children's experiences unfold outdoors. It uses the early learning standards to create a cohesive framework for advocating and acting on behalf of children's need for time in rich outdoor environments. It provides a pragmatic, real-time view of individual children pursuing their own questions and interests outdoors. By documenting and analyzing the content of their experiences, it reveals the multifaceted learning embedded in children's explorations and activities outside. Our hope is to inspire and excite you about the possibilities and opportunities that exist for children and for teachers outdoors.

The stories and photographs that fill this book were culled from hours of observing children engaging with the outdoor world in diverse settings through all four seasons of the year. We deeply appreciate the partnership we were afforded at settings large and small, rural and urban. School directors and teachers have been generous, open, and engaged with us in our work, sharing their sites and insights with us and letting us spend time observing, transcribing, and photographing their children's play. The creativity of the teachers depicted in these pages and their commitment to reconnecting children and nature are inspiring. It is their generosity and openness that has made it possible for us to explore and compile this rich body of material.

The most beautiful thing under the sun, is being under the sun.
CHRISTA WOLF

Learning in Nature

CHILDREN ARE quintessential experiential learners. It is in their nature to investigate, examine, and work to make sense of everything around them. Busy and alert, they are information gatherers, taking in and processing each sound, sight, and sensation as they encounter it. This highly motivated approach to exploring and understanding, so characteristic of young children, is a quality they bring with them wherever they go. It can be seen indoors as they work with blocks, look at books, and mix colors at the easel. It can be seen outdoors as they dig in the sand, run on a hill, and notice a butterfly. Children continuously respond to the sights and sounds around them. They are particularly sensitive to the many physical sensations that are part of these experiences.

The outdoors is particularly well suited to children's active-physical-sensory approach to learning, offering endless and diverse opportunities for them to interact with the environment. Children may hear the chirp of a cricket and stop what they are doing to listen. They bend to the shape of a tree as they lean against it. Feeling the sun on their shoulders, they move their bodies to gather its warmth. They instinctively seek shade on a hot day. Children use their whole bodies and all of their senses as they make discoveries about the world. They run, skip, sit quietly, crawl, dig, and lie on the ground. Mesmerized by seemingly simple things, they are eager to understand how those things come to be. They test ideas by watching and listening, experimenting, and pondering the results of their actions. They place leaf after leaf in a creek to watch how each one makes its way in the current. They work hard to fill a large bucket with sand and then empty it, over and over again. They follow a butterfly from flower to flower as it travels through the garden. They collect favorite rocks, colorful leaves, acorns, seedpods, and other natural objects until their pockets are full. Children in rich outdoor environments can stay busy all day long with little or no prompting from adults. Given ample time to explore and rich materials to discover, children and their outdoor environment function as a unit—inseparable and connected.

The Critical Role of Play in Children's Learning

Outside play is often valued primarily for its contribution to children's physical and social development. It is also seen as an opportunity for children to take a break. Learning is seen as different from play and is generally understood as something that happens indoors, in the classroom. Yet, if one applies the early learning standards directly to the content of children's play outside, what is revealed is that play and learning are one and the same. In addition, "such playful contexts typically provide an important motivational component in children's learning" (Pellegrini 1995, 88). Children develop extraordinary competence as they play with one another in self-initiated ways. This is particularly true of the long-term attitudes and learning dispositions that are the focus of this book. Attitudes like inventiveness, flexibility, curiosity, persistence, and resilience are learning dispositions that children develop and refine primarily through play.

The value of play is increasingly the subject of important research. The many skills children develop through play, particularly the self-control practiced and refined in imaginary play, are related to long-term academic achievement. "The ability of young children to control their emotional and cognitive impulses, it turns out, is a remarkably strong indicator of both short-term and long-term success, academic and otherwise" (Tough 2009, 32). Taking a closer look at children's play outside is essential to understanding what and how much children learn in outdoor environments. The early learning standards provide a lens through which it is possible to see children's learning more clearly. This book models how to use the standards to better see and evaluate children's learning experiences outdoors.

Play is the primary vehicle children use to explore and make sense of their world. Play is the means by which children engage with materials, ideas, and each other, testing out theories and refining their understanding. Often it is not until adults stop, observe, and reflect on the specific content of children's play that they realize how sophisticated children's work is. As Michel Montaigne explained in the year 1580, "Children at play are not playing about; their games should be seen as their most serious-minded activity."

Without a guide, it is easy to gloss over the details and miss the profound and serious nature of children's play, especially children's play outside. Children interact with and respond to their environment and to one another by playing with ideas and perceptions. They engage in make-believe as they take on the roles of mommy, daddy, doctor, and teacher. They build bridges, forts, houses, and towers. They invent games with sophisticated rules they have to explain to each other and regulate themselves to follow. They put on plays and create performances, becoming tightrope walkers, lion tamers, ballerinas, and bad guys. They pretend to do things they aspire to: they drive cars or buses, blast off into space as astronauts, lecture one another as they pretend to be the teacher, read books to one another, take care of sick animals and babies. In doing so, they sift through and test out information and perceptions, working together to build an understanding of the world. As Fred Rogers of *Mr. Roger's Neighborhood* explains, play gives children a chance to practice what they are learning. "They have to play with what they know to be true in order to find out more, and then they can use what they learn in new forms of play" (1983, 95).

The unique play experiences available to children in the natural world spontaneously call to their curiosity, their initiative, and their imagination. The questions they encounter there organically bring into play reasoning and problem solving. The challenges children overcome outdoors lead to greater persistence, confidence, independence, and an ability to engage appropriately with risk taking. Nature provides ongoing teachable moments, endless opportunities to make discoveries, and limitless reasons for critical thinking. The outdoors is a receptive place for children to apply and refine their developing skills through play.

Early Learning Standards Unfold Naturally Outdoors

The goals of early learning standards are to improve the quality of education for young children and to support teachers by identifying benchmarks in children's growth and development. Early learning standards are equally applicable to indoor and outdoor learning environments. However, most of the guidance provided for teachers about how to use them has, to date, focused exclusively on the indoors. The accountability they feel for incorporating standards into their teaching practice and the emphasis on the indoors of standards-based training has deterred many teachers from thinking of applying those standards outside. The result is a lack of understanding about the importance and effectiveness of using the outdoors to support children's learning and engagement with early learning standards. This book provides guidance in applying the standards from the approaches to learning domain to the outdoors. More importantly, by shifting the standards outside, this book offers a new and exciting lens for seeing what a powerful partner the outdoors is in children's learning.

An analysis of children's outdoor play and its content shows how their experiences engage them seamlessly with the content of the early learning standards, particularly the approaches to learning domain. The words used to describe children's behaviors and attitudes in approaches to learning—such as curiosity, imagination, problem solving, and risk taking—are the same words that describe children's outdoor play. The early learning standards and approaches to learning therefore point teachers strongly back to the context of the natural world. It is the ideal place for children to engage with and develop the important attitudes and skills the standards catalog.

Early learning standards are not static. They are not short-term measurable outcomes like learning objectives that can be tested, quantified, and checked off as completed on a child's learning profile. Rather, these critical long-term outcomes and behaviors need to be encouraged and supported because they significantly influence all future learning. Standards are dynamic: they are qualities, attitudes, and habits that teachers can promote and extend in children by planning environments that purposefully focus on them. The list of standards addressed in this book is provided in the appendix.

Increasingly, teachers in early childhood settings are recognizing the outdoors as a unique and essential site for learning and looking for ways to offer children more time and opportunity to play outside. This often involves rethinking children's daily routines and practices, then redesigning or improving their current outdoor space. Teachers in settings all across the country are at different stages of engaging with the outdoors. You may be in a setting in which you are already working hard to improve the quality of your outdoor environment. Or you may be working in a setting that seems to have limited opportunities for improvement. Whatever your situation, it is important to participate in this dialogue about the benefits of outdoor learning and to look for ways to help children reconnect with nature.

Look at your play yard to draw out the natural elements available there. Is there a tree children can adopt, learn about, and take care of? Is there a little space for a small garden? If not, is there room for a container garden or window box? Is there an area where children can dig, look for rocks, or observe worms and insects? Can you hang a bird feeder to invite more life to your outdoor space? Anything you can do to improve habitat and increase the diversity of plant and animal life in your immediate area is a benefit to you and to the children you work with.

In addition to your own space, look into the community beyond your play yard fence. Is there a park nearby? Is there a neighbor with a garden who would like to share it with the children? Are there interesting places to visit on a neighborhood walk? Elements of nature are available to everyone, everywhere—the sky, the moving clouds, the wind and weather, the sun and rain. Each of these elements creates opportunities for discovery and conversation. Even in restricted urban spaces, children can collect rainwater, play with their shadows, make a windsock, or grow vines on the building wall or fence. Each of these activities engages children importantly with the rules, systems, and elements of the natural world that are so critical to their understanding. At the same time, such activities support children's engagement with the standards and the indicators of approaches to learning.

Connecting Children to the Natural World

Feeling at home in the natural world and having time to explore it are critical conditions for children's healthy development. Often, experiences in nature enjoyed by children two generations ago are no longer readily available. Rapid development of urban and suburban spaces have fragmented and destroyed many of the natural spaces children used to claim for their play. Many vacant lots, big backyards, local farms, untouched fields, and forests are no longer there for children to use. Children's play yards and school grounds are increasingly contrived. Although the trend is beginning to change, nature is often the least represented element outdoors, replaced by climbing structures, mulch, pavement, and other artificial elements.

In addition to this dramatic loss of natural spaces, both in neighborhoods and at schools, there has been a marked cultural shift away from unstructured and unsupervised time for children to explore the natural world. More parents are working, which means more children are spending all day in supervised child care. The perception and tolerance of risk has radically changed as well. Most adults are no longer comfortable permitting children to explore and claim wild spaces for their daily play with neighborhood friends.

There is an ongoing retreat to the indoors—to screen time on televisions, computers, and video games. Families seek the comfort of air-conditioning in the summer, heat in the winter, and a perception of safety behind closed doors. Compounding this problem is the belief of many adults that children's learning will be accelerated by more time with technology. As a result, there is both less natural space outdoors for children to claim and use and diminished opportunity for children to use what outdoor space there is. "The disappearance of nature has become so commonplace around the world that Japanese children actually have a word for it—hiraku—which means loss of grass, trees, plants, and play areas" (St. Giermaine 1994).

In response to this loss, schools and early childhood settings have both an opportunity and an obligation to advocate for children and nature. Doing so not only benefits children, it also supports teachers in meeting the many demands currently placed upon them. Understanding the role of nature in children's development requires that you commit to developing and using rich outdoor learning spaces. Pairing early learning standards and outdoor learning is a powerful and effective way to address children's needs. Taking the standards outdoors enhances children's learning and, importantly, helps to meet the critical responsibility you have to help children reconnect to the natural world. The stories and images in this book document how seamlessly children respond to the natural world when given time and space to do so.

Developing rich and responsive outdoor learning environments requires an understanding of the important roles of time and diversity in children's outdoor play. The quality of interactive collaboration between child and environment depends directly on expansive time and the diversity of the materials and opportunities available (Moore and Wong 1997). Children are sensitive to feeling rushed; they need ample time to engage meaningfully with an idea or an activity. Hurry creates stress and limits the imagination. Children are reluctant to take on a big idea or project if it seems they will not have the time to pursue it fully. Many of their projects and discoveries require sustained periods of time to evolve to a satisfying level of complexity. It can take time for a child to settle on a particular question or to develop an idea they want to pursue. Children benefit from extended time to develop their ideas and to choose materials that will help them explore or express what they are interested in.

Some of the most satisfying projects shown in this book spanned hours, days, or even weeks. These projects include an element of flexibility, a relaxed coming and going that enables children to feel comfortable and respond to their own rhythms and interests. This quality is in keeping with what is known about young children and their needs. When they wander off or become fatigued in the moment, it does not necessarily mean that they have lost interest in the project. If they are allowed enough time to come and go, they often reengage with new energy and a fresh perspective. It is in the nature of young children to dip in and out of activities. This unique pattern of engagement means that young children are best supported by having sustained periods of uninterrupted time when they play and work.

The diversity of the opportunities and materials available for children is another critical factor that defines quality outdoor learning environments. Children respond to difference and need many choices. The outdoor environment must therefore offer a range of possibilities to explore and a variety of elements to work with. Individual children at different times need large and small spaces, bright and shady spaces, and places that are high and low. They respond to differences in color, texture, form, and shape.

By inviting nature back into the play yard, children are provided with exactly the diversity they need. Trees, shrubs, and flowers offer myriad parts and pieces to compare and contrast. Sticks, stones, bark, seedpods, flowers, stems, and leaves offer interesting shapes, textures, colors, and forms to explore and compare. Such objects, which change with the seasons, are endlessly interesting and offer children a wide choice to play with. The effects of time and weather on natural materials mean that objects such as seedpods and fallen leaves change from day to day as they rot, dry out, or blow away. Such ongoing change adds magic to the play yard and captures children's imagination. Providing tools and props such as buckets, shovels, magnifying lenses, costumes, books, balls, and art materials extends the range of choices available to children outside.

Children are all about finding out. The stories in this book document how well children are able to "find out" in nature. They push, poke, and question to know "what is going on here." The way they find out is by setting things in motion and experiencing a response. The natural world is a system with rules, consequences, and patterns that can be discovered because they are real. If children pay attention, look, listen, and feel, they can form their own questions and find clues that lead to real knowledge. With experience and diverse materials, they will gather the data that leads them to understand gravity and the fact that water always runs downhill. With enough time to themselves outside on bright spring days, children may discover the different patterns of bird songs and recognize a robin when it calls. Perhaps they will build a dam in a running stream, group rocks to slow the water down so that in that little calm spot ice miraculously forms over a chilly winter night. Children can see what happens all around them outside, and wonder why.

"Play not so much reflects thought (as Piaget suggests) as it creates thought" (Vandenberg 1986). The underlying patterns and rules that are a part of nature make it an ideal setting for children, who are learning how to learn. Children's contemporary experience provides too little play and open-ended exploration in nature. The narratives in this book illustrate how children naturally gravitate toward experiences that are rich in interest, meaning, and learning when their play outdoors is valued. Thoughtful provisioning by teachers, adequate time, and opportunities for dialogue are essential components of a responsive outdoor learning environment.

How to Use this Book

In compiling standards and indicators for use in this book, we began by looking at early learning standards now in place across the United States. Because the standards vary somewhat from state to state, we analyzed them for trends, commonalities, gaps, and overlaps. We synthesized the results of our research into a representative and comprehensive list of standards for the approaches to learning domain that is applicable and useful for all teachers.

We then looked at the observable behaviors states have framed as guidelines for teachers to use when applying the standards. Again, we looked for patterns and shared language. For each standard, we developed a representative list of age-appropriate indicators for three- to five-year-old children. The number of indicators representing each standard varies from three to five. The fact that some standards have more indicators than others is not because one standard is any more important than another. Rather it has to do with the number of essential behaviors required to capture what the standard looks like in action. A similar range exists in the number of indicators or behaviors different states assign to their early learning standards. As a result of this variance, chapter lengths differ according to the number of indicators assigned to the particular standard being discussed. In creating our list, we made indicators as clear, concise, and useful as possible (see the appendix on pages 201–203).

As you reflect on the indicators, always remember that each child is unique. Indicators will look different depending on a child's age, temperament, interests, abilities, work style, and background. As you read the narratives accompanying the indicators, remember that these stories are only a few examples of thousands that could be used to illustrate each indicator. The stories provide you with new tools for looking at your setting and new ideas for thinking about the children. Rather than telling you what to do, the narratives give you a springboard for thinking about how you can make it more likely that children will engage effectively with each standard. Early learning standards are a valuable tool encompassing and operationalizing current knowledge in the field of child development. The standards address all areas of a child's growth in an organized and comprehensive way. Taking them outside provides insight and guidance for the design of programs and activities and offers a new lens for observing children and their development in a meaningful way.

The goal of this book is to provide practical guidance in how to use the outdoors more consistently and effectively to support early learning. The outdoors provides an ideal environment for children to develop positive attitudes toward learning and to practice behaviors described in the early learning standards. The narratives build an essential bridge between the standards and the experiences of teaching and learning outdoors. By presenting real children outdoors engaging in powerful ways with the standards in their daily work and play, the narratives clearly show the link between children's responses to the materials and experiences available outdoors and children's growth as framed by the standards.

You may use this book in a number of ways. The examples and stories it contains provide ideas for activities, materials, and settings that will help anyone working with children outside. You can read it cover to cover as an enjoyable text and resource on outdoor learning. Or use it as a reference book to look up individual early learning standards and related topics. Each of the standards in the approaches to learning domain is discussed separately in its own chapter (chapters 2 through 8) and presented using a consistent structure:

- Introduction to the particular standard discussed in the chapter

- Overview: Why is this standard important for healthy child development?

- Pragmatic View: How do states and national early childhood organizations classify this standard?

- Applied View: What observable behaviors or indicators demonstrate this standard?

- Experiencing this Standard in the Outdoors: We provide two illustrated narratives for each indicator, each followed by a discussion of how the indicator relates to outdoor learning. The discussion includes an analysis and interpretation of the story. A discussion or reflection question is provided for each indicator.

- Further Reflection: How might applying this standard affect your teaching outdoors?

For every early learning standard, teachers look for observable behaviors indicating that children are engaging with the content of that standard. These observable behaviors are alternately called "indicators," "widely held expectations," "performance indicators," or "benchmarks" by different states. We have chosen the term "indicators" as the clearest name for examples of a particular standard in action.

We have synthesized the observable behaviors articulated in the various state standards for the approaches to learning domain into a representative list of age-appropriate indicators for three- to five-year-old children. These indicators manifest themselves in a myriad of ways and depending on numerous factors, including children's age, temperament, interests, abilities, work styles, and cultural context. Regardless of the unique learning style, background, and needs each child presents, the primary factors in how children experience each of the learning standards are the setting and materials you offer and the way you respond and attend to the children.

While this list of indicators is equally applicable to both indoor and outdoor settings, the focus here is on the outdoors. Our intent is to illustrate the distinctive ways rich outdoor environments are responsive to children's curiosity and initiative. We use two narratives to explore and depict each indicator. The stories provide an exciting glimpse into this special world and the potential it offers for teaching and learning.

We invite you to focus on the stories as illustrations and examples of quality outdoor learning. Reading about activities and teaching that have occurred in other settings may help you develop a greater appreciation for the opportunities that already exist at your own site. It may also help you think about how to extend and enrich those opportunities. You can put yourself in these stories and imagine what it is like to work with children in a well-provisioned outdoor environment every day. You can also begin to see how your own stories complement those we have provided here. Such discoveries are affirming and motivating. The stories reveal the multiple ways children learn outdoors. Reading them can expand the range of activities you provide to support children's learning. You may also choose to skip the words and concentrate on the images and the stories they tell.

We also encourage you to use this book to strengthen your voice in promoting and describing the benefits of outdoor learning in conversations with colleagues, parents, community leaders, and policy makers. By delving deeply into what children are actually doing outside and looking at their activities through the lens of the standards, we build a case for the essential role of outdoor learning. The central message of this book is that a critical connection exists between children's healthy growth and development and time spent outdoors. Much of the learning described here can happen nowhere else.

"That's funny," said Pooh. "I dropped it on the other side . . .

and it came out on this side! I wonder if it would do it again?"

And he went back for some more fir-cones.

A. A. MILNE

Curiosity and Initiative Standard

CURIOSITY AND INITIATIVE thrive in the outdoors because there are so many surprises for children to discover, changes for them to try to understand, sounds and movements that are unplanned, and opportunities for them to observe and experiment with cause and effect. Well-provisioned natural environments offer children encounters with real-life puzzles and problems. The outdoors is full of elements that constantly respond to changes in the light, weather, and seasons. Such an interesting and dynamic environment encourages children to engage in a continuous cycle of exploration. As you watch them, you can see how one experience leads to another; their curiosity prompts them to ask questions and their initiative leads them to investigate.

Overview

Why is the curiosity and initiative standard important for healthy child development?

Children are naturally curious. From the beginning, they show eagerness and a sense of wonder. Babies are born with a predisposition to use their senses to explore and understand the world around them. Years of discussion about nature and nurture have shed light on how children develop in relation to the environment surrounding them. It is the interaction between the child and the environment that enables learning to occur. Children are predisposed to try to "connect the dots" and make sense of their firsthand experience. They are motivated both by their natural curiosity and the inborn human drive to meet their needs. Therefore, the child and the environment are partners in the enterprise of learning and becoming a person. Curiosity is a major component that drives both children's exploration and the refinement of perception that occurs as they learn from the environment.

Like curiosity, children display initiative from the very beginning as they work to meet their needs. Initiative is both the active aspect of curiosity in which children move out into the environment, poking, pushing, and "doing things to find out," and a manifestation of the child's desire to have an impact, to "make a mark" on the world. You cannot create curiosity or directly teach children to be curious and show initiative. Rather, it is critical to find ways to work with these inborn traits and encourage, nurture, and extend these aptitudes in young children. You can best support children's interest in learning new things and trying new experiences by providing environments that offer rich materials and the opportunity to self-select activities and projects. This allows children to grow in their independence and develop their ability to make thoughtful, healthy, and rewarding choices.

The early childhood years are a time when important attitudes toward learning are formed and cemented for children. By providing young children with an environment designed to support them as they exercise their curiosity and initiative muscle, you help equip children with attitudes that will affect their learning in a lifelong way. When children feel supported by adults who are open to their desires to pursue questions and activities that interest and engage them as individuals, the result is powerful. Children experience what it means to be an active player in their own learning. They learn to observe the world in creative, expansive ways, formulate meaningful questions, and discover answers to their own questions.

Pragmatic View

How do states and national early childhood organizations classify curiosity and initiative?

When looking at early learning standards across the country, curiosity and initiative are among the standards most frequently mentioned. These two standards are the primary engines that drive children out into the world. Curiosity and initiative compel children to ask questions, initiate interactions, make choices, express interest, and direct their growing independence. These actions link children directly to the environment, which is the fundamental source of their learning. An analysis of the behaviors most states use as descriptors for curiosity and initiative reveals words that connote energy and striving:

- eagerness
- trying
- experimenting
- discovering
- expressing
- finding
- asking
- discussing

While curiosity is most often paired with initiative, it stands alone as a category in some states, while in other states it is paired variously with engagement, persistence, or eagerness. Similarly, initiative is usually paired with curiosity but some states have paired it with persistence, and in others it stands alone as its own standard. This speaks to the fact that curiosity, initiative, and persistence are three standards sharing many of the same qualities necessary to fuel healthy development. We pair curiosity with initiative because the two are so interrelated and are easier to understand together than alone. Curiosity is about the desire to know and initiative is about the ability to develop a plan that will let a person find out and satisfy his or her desire to know. By understanding these qualities and valuing them as important approaches to learning, you can encourage their further development. Talking with and listening to children as they describe and develop their ideas are critical skills for teachers to practice to promote curiosity and initiative in children. In addition, it is important to monitor and adjust the classroom environment in response to children's interests. This can include revisiting scheduling practices, routines, materials, centers, and activities.

Applied View

*What are the observable behaviors or indicators that demonstrate
children engaging with the curiosity and initiative standard?*

Curiosity and initiative are very powerful and enormously valuable forces that fuel children's learning. Because each is a driving force, they demand action. Children need and require things and materials to investigate, ask questions about, and explore. The environment is therefore a key player in supporting children's engagement with this standard. In planning the environment, teachers need to provide variety, choice, and ample time for children to explore and pursue their ideas. The outdoors, because it offers so many choices and provides space to explore them, is a great resource. In a rich outdoor environment, unplanned aspects of children's curiosity and initiative are less apt to become disruptive because the children are engaged and involved. Successful teachers celebrate and support unplanned directions that children's curiosity and initiative can take. They recognize these behaviors as instrumental in promoting children's learning. Standards highlight and clarify what to look for.

From the observable behaviors articulated in the various state standards, we have synthesized five indicators of curiosity and initiative for three- to five-year-olds:

1. The child demonstrates eagerness to learn by asking questions, developing ideas, and exploring objects and materials.

2. The child expresses interest in others and initiates interactions.

3. The child wonders about the world and is open to new experiences.

4. The child uses a variety of senses to explore the world and experience answers to questions.

5. The child invents projects and works on them with growing independence.

Experiencing the Curiosity and Initiative Standard in the Outdoors

INDICATOR 1: *The child demonstrates eagerness to learn by asking questions, developing ideas, and exploring objects and materials.*

THE RED LEAF

"Look it has a little hole in it so it hangs. Maybe it's part of the tree and it ripped, or maybe it came from another tree and fell and got stuck!"

After playing in the woods for fifteen minutes or so on a rainy day, Molly decides that she is feeling wet and cold and is ready to head back into the classroom with the group. On her way, she sees a lone red leaf suspended on a sapling. Its brilliant color stands out against the muted browns and

grays of the fall forest. She stops to examine it. She notices that it is hanging from a twig, not by its stem, but from a hole in the leaf. This simple puzzle immediately draws her into a world of wondering aloud, "What is going on here?" The first explanation that occurs to her is that the leaf is the last of the leaves that belong to the sapling and that it simply hasn't fallen yet because it is attached by the hole. She looks up into the trees overhead, many of them still holding some of their leaves, and sees something that leads her to question her initial explanation. With this new information, she develops an alternate hypothesis: she wonders aloud if perhaps the leaf came from a taller tree and was neatly captured by the twig on its way to the ground.

THE NATURAL WORLD is full of showstoppers like the red leaf that capture a child's attention and imagination. In addition to being beautiful in itself, the leaf is the result of an action (a leaf falling) and a process (leaves turn color in the fall). The act of observing it links the child to questions and clues about larger issues and natural phenomena. Once they enter this world and begin to investigate, children and their teachers discover what John Muir has described so well, that outside "when we try to pick anything out by itself, we find it hitched to everything else in the universe" (Muir 1911, 157). This holistic aspect of nature is what makes learning outdoors so natural and so fulfilling.

Molly found a puzzle and formulated a question that might explain what she was seeing. She tested out her hypothesis, refined it by adding new information, and continued to wonder about what was going on. The role of the teacher in supporting this inquiry process was essential. Giving the child a premature explanation would have closed off the natural process of inquiry she was engaging in, and that is necessary for building understanding. Providing children with the right answer can actually inhibit and discourage them from discovering, supposing, and proposing solutions of their own. By giving time and space for children to ponder what they are seeing and wondering about, teachers support curiosity and initiative and ensure that children will continue to formulate both questions and answers with confidence. Creating working propositions extends and sustains children's skills of observation and helps them look for interconnectedness in the world around them. Children's ability to truly engage in the process of inquiry is fundamental to all of their learning.

THE DEAD BIRD

"It's not dead. It's pretending. It's just scared," offers Jared.

"How will we know?" asks his teacher.

"Let's touch it with a stick or gently turn it over. If it's not dead, it will fly away," suggests Crosby.

"Oh . . . it's dead," concludes Josh.

Jared and his mother arrive late to school and on their way into the building they notice a dead bird lying in the leaves by the parking area. When they come into the classroom, Jared mentions what he has seen to one of the teachers. Very quickly, a group of interested children gathers to hear about it. Eight children go out with a teacher and her assistant to investigate this situation while the rest of the children happily continue with their work inside.

Before setting out, the teacher and children discuss some guidelines they will use in their investigation that will keep them all safe. These include just looking at the bird, not touching it, and staying far enough back that everyone can see. As they approach the scene, they form a semicircle around the bird, looking at it and wondering aloud whether it is really dead. They suggest they can find out by turning it over with a stick to see if it might fly off. Using a long stick, the teacher gently rolls the bird over and when the bird shows no sign of moving, they conclude that yes, it is dead. They then begin to look for clues to explain how it died. One child suggests looking for an injury or "hole" in the bird's side, and when none is found, they begin to take inventory of the area around the bird, looking for further clues.

"I think it was nesting up there and last night it got too cold.""Or the bumblebee stung it" (said as an insect flies by)."Look. Here's a clue" (pointing to a bush). "I think it got scratched here by the branches."

This lively discussion transpires with the children proposing different ideas, each incorporating different aspects of the surrounding environment to explain what might have happened. The children listen to one another and the teacher listens to each child. Sometimes she asks a question to clarify or extend their ideas. Once everyone who wants to share has spoken, one of the children proposes that they bury the bird.

These children are lucky enough to have a teacher who sensed the need for and supported the ritual they developed to express their powerful feelings. The children decide to bury the bird. Burial is a cultural expression of respect for the dead, and a tradition they have no doubt absorbed from stories and perhaps personal experience. But they go further, creating a song that helps express the strong feelings this experience has aroused in them. They sing their song both spontaneously and self-consciously, as if they are watching themselves and examining their own response as they are making it up.

"Let's bury it."

"I think we should bury it."

"We need a box."

"Let's sing a song . . . a sad song. One song while we're burying it and one after."

The children form a procession, each one singing a different song. They walk toward the nearby woods and bury the bird under a blanket of leaves. Josh sings, "We're sorry little bird that you are dead. We're sad little bird. But we need to bury you. We're sorry bird that we'll never see you fly." The last line of his song indicates Josh's awareness of death as the end of the cycle of life. He recognizes that the bird is no longer a part of the ongoing process around them.

Children ask teachers many questions about things they want to understand. When does it support children's learning to answer their questions for them? When does it interfere with children's learning for you to give them the answers?

THE OUTDOORS holds many unexpected puzzles that are deeply embedded in the environment and that encourage children to be observant and notice changes around them. These are mysteries to be unraveled and revisited within a growing understanding of how the world works. Changes outdoors are different from the changes children observe inside (which most often are the result of a decision and a conscious change made by an adult). Outdoors things happen without being planned by the teacher. The spider web the children discover on Monday is sparkling with dew when they see it again on Tuesday morning. Or it holds a struggling insect, or perhaps it has disappeared altogether. The dead bird nestled in the leaves at the edge of the parking lot is a mystery waiting to be discovered, or perhaps it will go unnoticed before the body is removed or eaten by another animal. It is a mystery with a life of its own. When noticed, it provides children with a window into a much larger, ongoing system: the cycle of life. Birth, life, and death occur all around us outside. They are there to be observed and wondered about in the plants, animals, and insects that share our world.

The experience of a dead animal and the examination of its body provide powerful inducements for children to ask questions. People are affected by the experience of death throughout life, and it continues to be one of life's great mysteries. The children's growing understanding of cause and effect was reflected in their questions; they understood both that the bird was dead and that something caused this death. They worked to refine their understanding by wondering aloud about the clues they found and using them to create and test various scenarios about how this might have happened.

Experiences like this are rich with meaning and emotion. Like throwing a pebble into a quiet pond, what happened here can be described as a single event, but it is not a self-contained event. The entry of the pebble into the pond generates rings of disturbance that travel great distances across the water—and sometimes back again. The feelings and ideas contained in the moment of confronting the dead bird will ripple out into future time, into other areas of the curriculum, and back and forth through these children's own life experience. They weave together cause and effect, life and death, movement and stillness, safety and danger in a way not easily learned in any other manner but this kind of firsthand experience. Children deserve the opportunity to make these discoveries in supportive environments where there is time and space to mull over and absorb the powerful lessons they teach.

INDICATOR 2: *The child expresses interest in others and initiates interactions.*

SCARF PLAY

"I have one green eye and one just regular eye."

Five children are playing in an urban outdoor space that has many props and tools easily accessible for them to use. They begin by inventing a game using musical instruments and movement to respond to music the teacher is

playing on their outdoor cassette player. Extending their involvement, several youngsters run to a bin and select colorful see-through scarves. Hailey ties a green scarf over her head, by chance covering only one of her eyes. After looking around and experimenting with what she sees, she says, smiling, "I have one green eye and one just regular eye." Tarik has been watching her and is intrigued by what she is doing. He wants to try it for himself to see what it is like. Covering your face with a translucent colored scarf can be exciting. Like putting on colored glasses, an orange scarf turns the world orange and a green scarf turns the world green. He drapes the scarf over his head but each time he begins to run, it floats away. Hailey notices his difficulty and offers to help. They work together to tie the scarf on his head just the way he wants it.

SENSORY PLAY, such as Hailey and Tarik's play with the scarves, can happen inside or outside. However, the outdoors, with its generally more expansive space and open sky, encourages faster and larger movements and louder voices than are comfortably accommodated inside. As a result, a greater range of behaviors in children occurs as they interact, explore, and learn outside. Some themes are more easily accommodated in the larger canvas of the outdoors. Superheroes and bad guys, for example, with their fast and dramatic movements, might be dangerous in the confines of indoor space, but outdoors, with little more than a cape, children can safely use their superpowers and "fly at cyber speeds" across the play yard as they confront their imaginary enemies together. The outdoor environment has the potential for offering children many choices, as well as time and space to follow their own inclinations.

More children spontaneously engage in dramatic play outdoors than indoors, where dramatic play is often confined to a specific area or activity. Outdoors, for instance, the space under the slide becomes a fairytale castle, the pocket behind the shrubs becomes a horse stable, and the wooden seat on the sandbox becomes a train. Children can be encouraged to initiate interactions with one another by the availability of costumes and props, and also by unplanned events, such as falling leaves or the movement of shadows. "Their fantasy play . . . is the main repository for secret messages, the intuitive language with which the children express their imagery and logic, their pleasure and curiosity, their ominous feelings and fears" (Paley 1988, vii). Teachers can design learning environments to encourage independence and interactions by including rich, varied, and accessible materials along with predictable protocols and routines. In such an environment, children are able to interact directly with both the materials and one another with minimal assistance from an adult.

In this particular interaction with the scarves, the children were able to notice one another's activities, build on each other's ideas, and develop new sequences of play. The result was a joyful interaction with both the music and with one another. Hailey and Tarik were sharing an experience that sensitizes them to one another. After watching her, Tarik became excited about what Hailey was doing with the scarf and, in turn, she was able to notice that he was struggling to join her in what she was doing. What made it possible for each of them to act on their understanding was that no teacher stepped in to solve the problem for them. Both children were able to take initiative: she was able to offer to help him and he was able to accept her help. This interaction demonstrates two important things. It enriched their connection to each other and it built in each of them a sense of their own competence in solving problems.

THE ZIPPER

"I can't do it. Will you help?"

It is a cold day and the children are grabbing jackets and hats from the hooks on the back porch of their school as they head outside to play. Madison quickly slips her arms into her jacket and zips it up. She then turns and notices Jayla, who has also put on her jacket by herself but is struggling in the cold to join the two sides of her zipper. Madison confidently offers to help, and then spends several minutes attempting to insert the bottom of the zipper into the slider to start the process. Unable to get the tricky zipper to cooperate, she turns to an adult.

"I can't do it. Will you help?" asks Madison. As she watches the adult put the two pieces of the zipper together so that Jayla can finish the job by pulling up the tab, Madison comments, "I can do it for myself but I can't do it for other people yet."

THE OUTDOORS poses challenges to children that differ from the more predictable and more constant conditions they find indoors. One of the distinctive dynamics of the outdoors is that children must dress for, and respond to, changes in the weather. Many learning opportunities are inherent in the complicated actions of putting on shoes, boots, jackets, mittens, gloves, and hats, all of which require practicing and refining fine-motor skills. Most early childhood programs work to encourage children to become increasingly independent in their ability to manage the clothing associated with different kinds of weather. Teachers sometimes experience managing clothing as a burdensome challenge because so many children need help at the same time. Nonetheless, getting dressed for the outdoors is a valuable opportunity for children to develop independence and to help one another in a purposeful real-world way. By watching the hustle and bustle around them, children are aware that if they wait for an adult to help, it will take longer to get outside. This motivates them to try to dress themselves so that they can get outside more quickly.

Most children have a natural interest in one another and want to interact. Their interactions emanate from shared needs, interests, experiences, and understandings. Madison recognized herself in Jayla's struggle. She herself needed help with her zipper a few months ago. Now that she could do it for herself, she was eager to demonstrate and share her new competence by helping others. Although the two girls had not been playing together, Madison responded immediately when she saw Jayla's frustrated efforts. While she was not yet able to succeed fully at the task, it was clear from Madison's statement to the teacher that she had set a goal for herself and was working toward accomplishing it. An environment that allows children to set such goals, and gives them opportunities to move along a continuum of skills at their own pace, supports authentic learning. It supports children who, like Madison, are self-starters who demonstrate initiative and responsibility in becoming independent learners.

A well-designed outdoor space supports children's independence by creating increased opportunities for teachers to spend time listening and observing children and their interactions with materials and one another. What kinds of things might you learn about an individual child if you had this time to really listen and observe?

THE CHICKEN

"Maybe she's laying an egg!" says Abby. "Look she's sitting down!" Turning to the chicken, she says, "Can you do one?" Looking at Carl, who is standing nearby, she continues, "Look, it might lay an egg! Good boy!"

Carl looks at Abby and quickly chimes in, "You mean 'Good girl!'"

Abby is fortunate to be able to observe a number of farm animals at her school, which has a small farm project on site. One day, as she participates in putting out feed for the chickens strutting about the little farmyard, she notices that one chicken is sitting quietly by itself in the straw. She walks over to take a closer look. She spends several minutes simply standing and observing the chicken. When Carl joins her, she shares her speculation that perhaps the chicken is sitting still on the straw because it is laying an egg. She then tilts her head to each side trying to see under the chicken to confirm her idea. Unable to see what is under the chicken, she speaks directly to it, saying, "Can you do one?" Then, turning to Carl, she shares her notion that the chicken may be laying an egg. When she refers to the chicken as a boy, Carl gently corrects her, adding his knowledge about chickens to the growing pool of information they are sharing.

CHILDREN are fascinated by animals and their behaviors, but increasingly, children today lack basic knowledge about plants, animals, and where their food comes from. Early childhood programs can help remedy this deficit by allowing children to tend gardens, care for animals, and spend unscripted time outside where they can experience the natural rhythms of life. Early childhood programs have a unique opportunity in designing their outdoor spaces to reconnect children and families with the natural world and give them daily opportunities to observe its processes. For example, while many children recognize wild and farm animals from the media and from occasional visits to zoos, farms, or parks, their understanding and knowledge about the lives and needs of these creatures are often superficial. In a rich outdoor environment—where children have access to dirt for digging; leaves for comparing; and butterflies, birds, and insects to notice and name—children can observe, ponder, and wonder about many things in the life cycle. Such an environment encourages them to be curious: to ask questions, experiment, check and recheck, and develop their ideas and understandings over time.

In this story, Abby had an idea about what chickens do. In particular, she had an idea about what this chicken might have been doing at that moment. She tried to verify her idea in a number of ways: by observing the chicken, by trying to see underneath the chicken, and by asking the chicken directly what it was doing. She also shared her proposition with Carl, inviting his participation in what she thought would be an exciting event. Abby was having a wonderful experience watching the chicken's small movements and noticing the wind ruffling the chicken's breast feathers as it tousled her own hair. She watched and wondered for a few minutes if indeed there would be an egg, and then moved on to another activity. Her question had not been answered, but in posing it, she was organizing and adding to her growing knowledge about living things.

THE MYSTERY OF THE VINE

Adrian's face expresses his bewilderment as he wonders, "What is going on here?"

Adrian has taken time out from running with his friends to sit in the shelter of a thornless climbing rose on a small raised platform at the edge of the other children's activities. As he sits, he reaches out with both hands to hold on to two of the thick stems that are in front of him. He is startled when the vine in his left hand unexpectedly shifts in his grasp, while the other offers the sturdy handhold he expects. He peers up into the tangle of vines over his head, moving the vine back and forth in his hand. Slowly, his gaze follows the stem back down to the ground, to the place where the vine has been severed from the root.

ON THE FACE OF IT, this is not one of nature's more dramatic stories. And yet, it bears a closer look. It is a beautiful illustration of some of the simple and unexpected experiences children have outside; experiences that help them notice patterns and understand systems. By spending healthy chunks of time outside daily, children develop an intimacy with the elements of their outdoor space. Over time, they deepen their understanding of their immediate environment and how it works. They notice changes, seasonal and otherwise. As part of their experience, they naturally seek to explain what they think is going on, and make predictions about what will happen next. The outdoors presents children with opportunities to notice and learn about unifying concepts through firsthand experience, concepts such as the force of gravity, the effects of rainfall, erosion, plant and animal adaptations, seasonal change, and weather systems. The outdoors offers teachers and children a living textbook for scientific discovery.

Adrian experienced a surprise. Surprises, puzzles, changes, and incongruities are motivating to children because they are curious to understand the discrepancy between what they expect to experience and what they are encountering (Kagan 2002). Adrian could tell by holding the two vines that they were different. The vine in his left hand was not anchored in the way he expected it to be, and it was behaving differently from the one he was holding in his other hand, which was stable and firm. This set him to wondering. He began to look around for clues that would explain why one was different from the other. First, he looked up to see if the vine was still connected to the arbor over his head. When he saw that it was, he experimented by moving the vine back and forth, tracing its path down the length of the stem, his eyes finally arriving at a straight cut through the stem that had separated it from its roots. He pushed and wiggled the stem a few more times to confirm that it was no longer attached. It was Adrian's understanding of the normal growth pattern of trees and shrubs that enabled him to identify this loose stem as an abnormal situation and to wonder about it. By posing some questions and experimenting with the stem, Adrian was able to compare this situation to others he had encountered and locate in the environment an answer to his question about what was going on. Discoveries like this one happen often outside, quietly and without conversation, the result of an intimate and ongoing dialogue between a child and the environment.

How do your feelings and attitudes about being outdoors support or hinder a child's ability to experience wonder?

INDICATOR 4: *The child uses a variety of senses to explore the world and experience answers to questions.*

SWEET STEVIA

"I like the Stevia best because it's sweet . . . it was growing somewhere here."

Fall has come. With the cold weather, many of the lush green plants in this school's "Taste Me" garden are no longer thriving. Michael, wanting to show a visitor his favorite plant, the Stevia, approaches the garden bed where he knows it was growing and begins to search for it. He looks for it, bending closely over the bed and looking carefully at the leaves of the different plants growing there. He touches each plant, feeling the texture of the leaves. Not satisfied, he leans forward to smell some of the plants to help him in his identification. Finally settling on one possibility, he picks a leaf and tentatively nibbles its tip. He considers it for a moment and then exclaims, "No, that's not it!"

IN WESTERN CULTURES people tend to exchange and gather information primarily through looking and listening. This limits sensory experience and the ability to process and understand what is encountered. The fact that children learn best when they engage with their whole bodies and all of their senses is captured in the ancient Chinese proverb, "I hear and I forget. I see and I remember. I do and I understand." Often children don't get a chance to engage physically and use one or two of their senses at a time. This deprives them of the full range of experience they need to learn and grow. Beyond the infant years, moving and sensory experiences such as smelling, tasting, and touching are often discounted as valuable ways to explore and gather information about the world.

Adults must be concerned about children's safety. However, they must be equally concerned about children's learning, which necessarily involves some risk. Since moving, tasting, and touching are natural behaviors and essential learning tools, children are always using them to engage with the world. You need to anticipate this, plan for it, and help children develop strategies to keep themselves safe while still allowing them to use these important ways of knowing. With your guidance, children can, over time, develop judgment about their own safety and become more capable and independent as they apply their curiosity and initiative in the world. One way to help children learn about safe ways to use their senses is to provide an opportunity for them to practice these behaviors in the more controlled situation of a tasting garden, such as the one at Michael's school.

Michael had a memory of a plant he enjoyed in the past from his school's tasting garden. Last season, he helped prepare the beds, cared for the plants, and made many discoveries about how each of the different plants in the garden felt, smelled, looked, and tasted. In the story, he returned to a garden that had been transformed by frost and drought into a mass of sticks, stems, and dry leaves—a seemingly undifferentiated mass of brown and gray matter with no discernible identity. When gardens reach this dormant stage, most adults turn their backs on them and simply wait for next year's growing season. Michael, however, had a different response. He displayed a strong curiosity about what was still growing and took the initiative to explore this changed landscape. He was highly motivated to find the Stevia, and was seemingly unperturbed by the changes he saw. He focused on the few green leaves he could find and marshaled his skills to tease out clues that would be missed by a less motivated investigator. Had he relied only on sight and sound, Michael would not have been able to make highly accurate distinctions between the plants. By relying on a broader repertoire of sensory exploration, one that included touch and, ultimately, taste, he was able to reach an accurate conclusion and find the Stevia he was looking for.

SHAVING CREAM STUDY

"I'm making chocolate!" Terrel says to a playmate. "It needs more shaving cream. I need to stir it."

Terrel is on his school's outdoor water deck, an inviting space where he has access to paintbrushes, spoons, mixing bowls, hand mixers, whisks, a tea kettle, buckets, bowls, an easel, and several different surfaces to work on. He begins by putting a little paint into a plastic bowl. He then becomes interested in changing the texture of the paint by adding some shaving cream to thicken the liquid. He adds more paint and then more shaving cream, alternating small amounts of each as he mixes them together with a long paddle. He uses, in turn, all the available colors of paint and continues to add shaving cream until the can is empty.

THE OUTDOOR ENVIRONMENT allows children to have deeper sensory experiences than are generally possible inside. It provides a stress-free and spacious studio space where experimental activities can be encouraged and easily cleaned up. It is the perfect place for children to use all their senses to experiment with materials that have the potential for being messy. They can smell the paint and shaving cream, hear the squishing of mud and clay, and feel the temperature and smooth surface of the table as they spread paint with

their hands. When spilling paint is not a problem, and their teachers are not trying to contain the work and the messiness to a restricted location, children can expand their play and integrate a range of materials, including natural objects like pinecones, sticks, sand, leaves, and mud. When paint is mixed with dirt, sand, or ice, the new combinations lead to new sensory discoveries. Imagine what it feels like to paint on the knobbly surface of a pinecone or on a smooth, weathered stick. Each medium responds differently to various materials. Through such experiences, children learn unscripted lessons about texture, color, and form.

Terrel initiated a number of small experiments. Absorbed in the physical process of stirring and mixing and getting more, he used his senses to find out what it felt like when he added more shaving cream and what it looked like when he added more paint. These were not experiments designed by a teacher, but rather explorations that he designed on his own in response to the materials that his teachers had set out. The generous array of materials and tools encouraged him to try different things and be involved with the process rather than solely focusing on the outcome or product at the end. He formulated his own questions and discovered his own answers. Children are naturally curious, which makes them natural scientists. Given a rich environment and the freedom to explore, they use materials in sophisticated ways to pose and answer their own questions.

What particular elements or qualities of the outdoors encourage children to investigate with all of their senses?

INDICATOR 5: *The child invents projects and works on them with growing independence.*

ICE WORKS

Madison is puzzled. She seems to wonder, "Why can't I get this leaf out?"

Madison begins her day by turning the compost barrel with a teacher in the morning. Together they discover a plate of ice that formed overnight on top of the barrel around a cluster of brown leaves. She picks it up and runs with her treasure to the clay table nearby and begins trying to extract one of the leaves from the frozen bundle. As she works, she notices the clay on the table and begins to form a plan to print the leaf onto the clay. Having this plan in mind makes it all the more important for her to be able to pull out a whole leaf, which is hard to do.

After trying several times, she goes looking for another source of leaves. She checks the birdbath to see whether the water there has also frozen overnight. Reaching in, she discovers a disk of ice, but finds that it has no leaves embedded in it. When she returns to her project at the clay table, enough time has passed that the ice has begun to melt and she is able to extract a long thin leaf of the willow oak. She lays this leaf across the smooth surface of the clay and uses the green roller to make an impression of it. She then peels away the leaf and examines her work. Satisfied, she sprays the surface with water and erases the image, ready to print again.

OUTDOOR ENVIRONMENTS are full of wonderful opportunities for spontaneous discoveries that require no direct teacher planning. In this narrative, the previous day's rain combined with freezing overnight temperatures resulted in a number of different and very exciting changes to investigate on the play yard. Rain and leaves froze into an intricate mass in the compost bucket, water in the birdbath froze into a spectacular fractured disk, and rainwater sitting on

the indented tops of overturned project buckets had frozen into nutlike shapes tinted with the red paint that had dried on the bucket. Each of these ephemeral treasures held a story about how it came to be and provided exciting new materials to explore and work with. The teachers here appreciated the potential of these unexpected icy offerings and supported the children's desire to explore them. They shared the children's excitement and took the children's lead in what they might like to do with them. Unscripted moments such as these are the hallmark of outdoor environments. Combined with skillful teaching, such occurrences allow children to invent their own projects, follow their own inclinations, and make their own discoveries.

Madison had a big idea. She pursued her idea through a number of different iterations. First, she found the ice. She became interested in the leaves trapped inside the ice and decided to try to take them out. While doing this, she noticed the clay, which she came back to later as a material to help her explore the nature of the leaf. When she was unable to free an entire undamaged leaf, she left the table and went to look for more ice, perhaps assuming that it would hold a more accessible leaf. Her idea about the birdbath also holding frozen water was correct but her investigation showed that there were no leaves inside this ice. Undeterred, she returned to the table to try again with the original ice mass. By this time, her original piece of ice had begun to melt, allowing her to extract a leaf and complete the project she had planned.

This elaborate sequence had many parts, each of which required different skills and materials. Madison was able to follow her idea through the physical space of her play yard, bringing the ice from the compost bin and the birdbath to the worktable. She was able to initiate a set of activities to explore her questions because the school environment is structured to support the children's efforts and interests. Key among the provisions that supported Madison's work

was the project table set out with various open-ended materials and tools. Because this project space is readily available, children can use it independently in creative ways as they explore their own ideas and pursue their own projects.

WATER WORKS

"We can use this for a flag."

Kiri is excited. She has found a branch on the play yard and wants to plant it in the sand area as a flag. As she begins to do so, she exclaims, "This gives me an idea!" She turns to Tarik and says, "Hold it and I'm gonna be right back." She returns with a shovel, and asks Tarik to hold the branch while she shovels. When he declines, she tries on her own, holding the branch in one hand while shoveling with the other. She then proudly announces, "I planted this tree!" With a friend's help she then turns on the hose to water her new "tree."

As the water streams gently down toward them, she says, "Dig, dig, dig, dig—it's coming through the water. It is coming through my shoes" and grabbing the branch, she quickly transplants it to a new spot at the end of

the sand area. There, she is joined by a number of new friends to plant it in a high mound. Watching the water approach, one of them says, "The water will get upper and upper and knock that tree down." A boy notes, "The water is coming! It's getting closer! We need this rock to block the water!" The group begins gathering rocks to block the oncoming water.

Kiri then announces, "We should dig holes for the water!" and the group begins to dig holes and trenches all around the mounded "tree" to capture the water's flow. "We should make deep holes! Make it go in my hole!" Kiri, at this point, leaves the group and goes to her cubby, quickly

returning and saying, "Look, I got my boots on so I can go in. I like to be wet!" She walks into the water, moving rocks and logs and extending their trench network all around the tree, still safely situated on its sandy mound.

THE OUTDOORS provides children with a rich canvas for the imagination, where materials and discoveries inspire narratives and projects in which many children can join and contribute to the story. Many of the projects children create for themselves unfold over a period of days, responding to new elements and to different children's ideas. This particular story begins with nothing more than a branch; by the end, the children have created a whole world in which the branch has been transformed into a majestic tree situated on a protected mound at the center of a raging river. In their miniature world, the children are replicating streamside erosion. Just as in a canyon where erosion can dislodge a tree, the water in the sandbox can sweep away the mound of sand and topple the tree the children have placed on top of it. This kind of project engages children directly with physical science—with materials and processes of the natural world—at a scale that they can understand and apply.

Kiri's project started with a little idea and a small action. In planting her branch, her idea expanded with the context and became part of a much larger scenario. The water and its action became prime players in the story that unfolded. As more and more children became involved and responded to the water's action, they shared their ideas about how to protect the tree and the play became increasingly complex. The fantasy of the tree on the bank was soon replaced by a real encounter with the water in which the children tried to control its flow. Because they had a real-world problem to pursue, with discoverable rules and parameters, the children were motivated to formulate ideas and devise solutions they could try out on their own. The natural world consistently provides all the materials and tools children need to pursue their questions about it. This enables teachers to observe children's actions, listen to their language, and assess their understandings, rather than direct their play.

How might the learning be different when a child develops and carries through his or her own project compared to completing a project you design?

Further Reflection

How might applying the curiosity and initiative standard affect your teaching outdoors?

While these narratives provide only a small sample of the ways the outdoors engages children's curiosity and initiative, they all portray the excitement and creativity that permeates children's activities outdoors when they have both unstructured time and open-ended materials to explore. In each story, children are deeply engaged by their encounters with real materials and the opportunity to formulate and answer their own questions. When you take the time to follow closely the thread of a child's thinking and reflect on what it is children are actually doing outside, you begin to see that children's constructions of the world are sometimes quite different from ours as adults. This is as it should be. Children are evolving their understanding of the world. To fully develop this understanding, children must have the freedom to work through their ideas over time and over many different encounters. By providing an environment in which questions can be explored, you encourage and support the healthy development of children's curiosity and initiative. Over time, these predispositions become habits of mind, long-term attitudes toward learning that equip children for success.

The important thing is not to stop questioning . . .
ALBERT EINSTEIN

Engagement and Persistence Standard

THE WORD "engagement" carries with it the sense of both connection and commitment. For example, when a couple becomes engaged, it implies that they are deeply connected, focused on each other, and eager to sustain and nurture that connection. Similarly, when children are truly engaged with an idea, with materials, with an activity, or with another child, they are focused and actively cultivating that connection. This wanting to "stick with something" is what persistence is all about. When children care about what they are doing, they stay with it and are willing to overcome distractions, difficulties, setbacks, and challenges.

The outdoors supports this standard because the natural world is a place defined by connection. Everything is connected to everything else. Children love to be outside where they feel a natural connection to everything: plants, animals, clouds, water, rocks. . . . When the milkweed blooms, the monarchs appear. When the weather turns cooler in the fall, the birds fly south. When the rain falls, puddles collect. With little effort, the outdoors unfolds itself to children and invites them to simply choose how they want to engage with it.

Overview

Why is the engagement and persistence standard important for healthy child development?

Children are active, concrete learners. They learn best in situations that are hands-on and that enable them to investigate, ask questions, and devise possible solutions. It is natural for children to demonstrate engagement and persistence as they interact with the world, provided that the environment encourages these behaviors. Infants, from the earliest days, notice and begin to track movement; the environment engages them from the start. As children grow, the environment continues to engage them, especially when it provides open-ended materials for them to investigate, extended periods of uninterrupted time in which to follow their ideas, and the opportunity to make choices. And of course, they need adults who support their engagement by being observant, asking the right questions, providing needed materials, and being interested in the questions they are exploring. This less-directive but more-involved role of the educator is especially effective outdoors where children have so many choices of how, and with what, to engage.

Engagement and persistence develop in company with each other and have to be encouraged in order to become lifelong habits. Once the stage is set for engagement, persistence begins to emerge. For example, children engaged in designing and building their own bridges with blocks may come back to the project for days, trying new designs and seeking out the perfectly shaped block to complete their idea. They may negotiate sophisticated trades with other bridge builders to make their concept work. Instead of giving up when they come up against difficulties, children dig deeper, try harder, and begin to invent ways to solve their problems. They may try alternate solutions or seek help from a friend or an adult. Among the benefits of persistence is the increased motivation for language development—as children are compelled to communicate about what they need and what they are thinking, they are willing to work to find words for what they are discovering. Children's engagement and persistence are mutually reinforcing. Practicing these behaviors at an early age ensures that children will have them as habits and attitudes for learning later in life.

Pragmatic View

How do states and national early childhood organizations classify engagement and persistence?

Along with curiosity, persistence is the early learning standard most frequently mentioned by states. It is frequently listed by itself, but when paired with another standard, it is most frequently paired with engagement. Engagement on its own is rarely listed. It may be that many states use persistence as a proxy for engagement. It is likely that some teachers assume persistence to include engagement. This is understandable because the two are so closely connected. However, there is benefit in pulling them apart, looking at the contribution each makes to children's development and how they relate to one another. Looking at engagement on its own helps teachers focus on how the environment calls to individual children: what materials, activities, and projects captivate a child's interest. This helps with planning and structuring the environment in ways that respond to and support children's needs.

Persistence, an outgrowth of engagement, provides a way to look at how a child is learning to focus and develop a sustained interest in particular projects or ideas. Persistence is recognized when children stay with a task over a period of time, add new and complex elements to their work, overcome obstacles, work through frustration, and manage distractions. Persistence is a standard that is difficult for teachers to take head-on. It is not possible to create persistence in children. However, you can set the stage for it by providing the right environment for engagement. Once children are engaged, they will want to stay with what they are doing—in short, to persist.

Applied View

What are the observable behaviors or indicators that demonstrate children engaging with the engagement and persistence standard?

The persistence and engagement standard is, at its core, a call to teachers to focus on the environment. Provisioning the learning environment with a variety of materials and activities offers children the opportunity to make choices and pursue a range of interests. An environment rich in materials and diverse activities and projects provides the requisite starting point to captivate each child's interest. Children presented with this diversity, and the necessary tools and time to investigate and pursue activities fully, become engaged. Their engagement supports and motivates them to pursue challenges, overcome obstacles, and persist through setbacks and distractions. In this way, they develop their ability to focus, stay with, and extend a project. The outdoor environment is ideal for engaging children. It is rich in changes for them to notice and investigate, presents puzzles to figure out, and has a range of both active and quiet activities to pursue. Enhancing the opportunities the natural world offers helps create an environment that calls to each child and to each child's interests.

Some of the phrases used to describe behaviors in the various state standards related to persistence and engagement are *sustained attention, purposeful planning, use of tools in ways that extend experiences,* and *the ability to work through challenges and obstacles.* These observable behaviors are captured in the list of indicators we have synthesized from the various state standards for both engagement and persistence.

Five observable behaviors are articulated in the various state standards for both engagement and persistence for three- to five-year-old children:

1. The child concentrates on a variety of age-appropriate tasks, activities, and projects despite distractions or interruptions.

2. The child pursues increasingly complex tasks, projects, and activities, willingly working on them over a period of hours or days.

3. The child continues to attempt a difficult task, sustaining attention and working through attendant frustration, disappointment, difficulties, and obstacles.

4. The child purposefully chooses activities and interactions of interest, develops a plan, and follows through with increasing independence.

5. The child seeks and accepts help, information, tools, and materials from peers and adults when needed.

Experiencing the Engagement and Persistence Standard in the Outdoors

INDICATOR 1: *The child concentrates on a variety of age-appropriate tasks, activities, and projects despite distractions or interruptions.*

PUZZLE GIRLS

Emma works steadily at her puzzle, testing the fit of each piece. "Does this go here?" she wonders.

It is a warm summer day. The teachers have decided to take a number of different center activities outside, including musical instruments, books, and chart paper with markers and puzzles. Emma goes directly to the puzzle table, finds a seat, and starts to work on the challenging puzzle of a train. Jelani stops at the music station and then approaches Emma. She watches Emma work for a few moments. Emma looks up at her with a smile and Jelani sits down beside her and picks up some puzzle pieces. The two girls of different abilities work in parallel for some time, one quite able to fit the

pieces together and the other engaged but not able to discover patterns to make the pieces fit. Each is focused on her own work. Emma's enjoyment of her success is evident on her face; she works steadily and confidently, undistracted by Jelani's different approach and level of skill. When a third child joins the table to work on the same puzzle, Emma greets him and includes him in the ongoing work, remaining focused despite this further interruption.

MANY TEACHERS find that children who do not normally choose certain activities indoors are more likely to try them if they are offered outside. Outdoors, children have a chance to observe activities from a distance, come and go from them in shorter spurts, and leave more easily if they become frustrated. This is because the outdoor environment is all of a piece, and a child does not have to be formally engaged in an activity to belong, to be engaged with something. Stepping away from a "center," the child is still in the midst of a shared space of sunlight and shadow and is still participating with others in feeling the wind and watching the clouds. The natural world offers a holding environment that always cradles the child. The result is that children generally feel less pressured outdoors than in. Outdoors there is generally more space, sound is not as concentrated and is therefore less distracting, there is more freedom to move about as they work, and there is always something new and unexpected to discover.

Engaging with the same puzzle in two very different ways, both Jelani and Emma were working with the task at their own developmental level. Jelani was exploring the pieces, feeling them with her hands and looking at their shapes, comparing them by putting one on top of another to see whether they matched. Emma, on the other hand, was working at a more complex level, successfully assembling the pieces of the puzzle, identifying by sight the pieces that fit together. Even though they were engaged in their own ways and at their own levels, each child was absorbed in her own exploration, undistracted by the activity of the other. Perhaps it is because they were outside that both these children approached this activity in such a comfortable, open-ended way. Children seem to be willing to use materials in less conventional ways and to take more risks with their learning outside than they might indoors. It could be that they feel less pressured by the oversight of adults and other children. It could also be, as research indicates, that the multisensory nature of the outdoors actually helps children focus (Taylor, Kuo, and Sullivan 2001).

Whatever the reasons, children's greater willingness when outdoors to try new things translates into active engagement. When children are truly engaged, they choose increasingly to return again to ideas and materials, work at deeper levels, and work through some of the difficulties that the materials may have presented. Such purposeful commitment is what defines persistence; committing purposefully to an activity leads to persistence, enabling children to develop it as a habit that is then transferred to other aspects of learning, both indoors and out.

SQUIRREL CACHE

"Do they wear socks?"

William's small group and several parents are on a field trip to a local nature center. The purpose of the visit is to investigate how different animals find food and shelter and manage to keep themselves warm in the wintertime. William wonders aloud if perhaps squirrels wear socks to keep warm. Other children share their ideas during a group discussion, reflecting their many different levels of understanding. The parents and children then bundle up and go outside for a directed walk in the snow to look for evidence of animals that are living in the frozen landscape.

The nature center's environmental educator leads the group, directing everyone's attention to specific objects and conditions found along the trail. William sees a small vine poking up through the snow and stops to investigate. He bends down and grasps it with his mittened hand. Scraping some snow aside, he uncovers a pinecone. He kneels down and digs further to expose a whole collection of pinecones, nut shells, twigs, and seeds. Working methodically, he exposes an area twelve inches in diameter. Keeping his head down, he continues to work away as his teacher and his mother both call his name and instruct him to rejoin the group.

THE OUTDOORS is full of subtleties and rich in secrets for children to uncover. Because the natural world is a system of real relationships and meaning, there is much that children can discover and learn on their own. Unless adults observe children closely, it is possible to miss the big ideas that children are engaged with as they investigate their environment. Discoveries such as William's squirrel cache in winter, bird nests and frog eggs in spring, acorns in the fall, or a visiting butterfly in summer are compelling entries for children into the workings of the natural world. It is important to recognize the powerful role of the environment in children's learning. When children are allowed to formulate and find the answers to their own questions, they become invested in their own learning and more persistent in finding answers. You can support and extend this wonderful interaction between children and place by keenly observing and tuning in to their activities and interests.

The indoor discussion about animals in winter set the scene for the children and sparked their interest in the specific problem of how animals stay warm in winter. As a result, they put on their coats and headed outside with great excitement to look for signs of animals and their winter activities. William acted with exactly the focused inquiry teachers mean to encourage. He had his three-year-old eyes peeled for clues of animal activity, and when he inadvertently uncovered the storage cellar of the gray squirrel, he knew he had made a valuable discovery. He was understandably eager to stay with it and see what was going on.

Moments like this can be hard for adults to both notice and correctly interpret. William was so absorbed in his work that he chose not to respond to the adults who were calling him to join the group. The adults were so caught up in leading the group and looking themselves for signs of wintering animals to show the children that they inadvertently missed William's discovering precisely what they came outside to find. Because the outdoors is so full of wonders that children can uncover for themselves, it is often best to frame a question of great interest, as this educator did inside, and then let children pursue it in their own way. Adults can then circulate among the group, supporting the different directions the children's discoveries may take, and help the children share with one another: "Come see what William has found!"

Young children are often characterized as having short attention spans. What in these two stories enables the children to stay focused and engaged for a long period of time?

INDICATOR 2: *The child pursues increasingly complex tasks, projects, and activities, willingly working on them over a period of hours or days.*

POTATO STORY

"Good luck. I hope you grow. Bye."

It is early spring. The teacher puts *Two Old Potatoes and Me* by John Coy (2009) out on the featured books table and calls the farm supply store to see if the seed potatoes are in. When they arrive, she displays the beautiful red and white potatoes in a large basket. The children investigate their smell, texture, and shape, and notice the little bright yellow-green sprouts already forming in some of the eyes. A group of boys and girls take big shovels, hand rakes, and trowels from the hooks on the side of the garden space and dig out the weeds in last year's potato bed, turning over the rich black soil. "Teeny weeds we can work into the soil, the orange pumpkin we can work in, the other weeds go in the bucket," says the teacher. Soon the bed is ready for planting.

The next day, planting day, is very cold and icy. The children gather around an outdoor table to cut the potatoes into pieces, each of which contains one sprout. The children put the pieces back in the basket and move over to the planting area. Placing their shovel tips to the frozen soil, the children ask, "How do we mix it when it's icy? It is popsicle dirt!" They each dig a hole in the resistant soil. "This is hard work." They place their seed potatoes in the hole with the green sprouts facing up, cover and then mound soil over them. After watering the mounds, the children mark their potato hills with a sprig of rosemary supplied by the teacher. Kiri asks, "Where is the sign? Let's make a sign. It should say, 'Only potatoes.'" Kiri and Madison head inside and make a sign. The teacher laminates it, and the next day all the children gather to "plant" the sign in the garden. "Good luck. I hope you grow. Bye," whispers Kiri to the potato hill as she walks away.

IN THE OUTDOORS, children experience the seasons and the passage of time in a tangible, accessible, and memorable way. They feel the temperature change, they get wet in the rain, and they notice the fluttering leaves falling to the ground. Each of these small experiences registers and leaves an impression that helps build each child's growing understanding of the rhythm of the seasons. Because of this, the outdoors provides a particularly suitable environment for longer-term projects and experiences where children can witness growth and change as it occurs, and can begin to make sense of it.

In this story, the children were in the early days of an experience outdoors that will command and sustain their attention over the whole span of the spring and summer. Longer-term projects such as this one provide ideal opportunities for children to develop and apply persistence as they follow the evolving and dramatic story of growth and harvest over a season. Here, the children's interest was focused by a compelling story in a book in which a little boy finds two old potatoes and wonders about the sprouts. Their interest grew when the teacher provided real seed potatoes like the ones they saw in the book and gave the children a chance to touch and investigate them. In structuring the garden work, the teacher provided a safe way for the children to cut their own potato sections to plant. She wisely made space and time for all the accidental and unplanned discoveries and experiences that accompany digging in the dirt to prepare the bed. The children found worms, uncovered an old potato just like in the book, and explored the remnants of a rotting "mushy" pumpkin, including its thick woody stem and slippery seeds.

The teacher was also receptive and open to the children's own ideas of how to extend the project. When Kiri suggested they needed a sign, the teacher understood this as an indicator of deep involvement. She captured the moment and released Kiri and Madison to go inside to make the sign. By laminating it, and creating time for the children's ceremony around planting it in the garden, she reinforced their initiative and supported their engagement.

Children develop persistence by being engaged in activities that inspire them. By offering the children so many different entry points into this activity, their teacher capitalized on the inherent excitement of growing potatoes, and engaged children with a wide range of interests and attention spans. She captured the imagination of diggers, observers, weeders, waterers, readers, and writers. Everyone was connected and will continue to have opportunities to be engaged, right up to the harvest and cooking of the first baby potatoes in the summer, right through the final harvest in the fall.

KITTY HOUSE

"We're kitties. We're zap kitties. If I zap him, he becomes a kitty. This is our kitty door. You're the mom and I'm the baby. I'm sharpening my claws. Kitties sharpen their claws on bark!"

"Kitty house play" has been popular with this group of children from the beginning of the school year. Almost every day children build small nests and dens inside the classroom where they engage in pretend play being

kitties. In November their play extends to being kitties outdoors as well, with most of the group participating. Perhaps inspired by the rustic outdoor shelter where they often have snack and read books, they decide to build an outdoor kitty house. Gathering materials from the forest floor, they work together over a period of months to construct and maintain a large stable structure that supports their play. Part of the play involves taking on the attributes of real kitties: Lucas is sharpening his claws on the bark of a nearby tree. Zach, finding a cozy patch of sunlight streaming through the roof of the house, stretches luxuriously and curls up in a ball for a kitty nap.

CHILDREN'S IDEAS, games, and imaginative play often move from the indoors to the more expansive stage provided by the outdoors. Why does this happen? The outdoors lends itself particularly well to extended projects that benefit from a lot of space or that need a longer stretch of time to be completed. Nature offers a diversity of open-ended materials children can use in a variety of ways. Because it is usually not necessary to take everything down and put things away at the end of each day outside, children are able to add to their projects over time. The ability to follow an idea through time and space often provides ongoing opportunities for problem solving, decision making, and communication between children. In the case of the kitty house, the wind and rain over the weekend had damaged the structure and the "kitties" spent several days discussing, repairing, and reconstructing their home.

Most children love designing and constructing things, making places of their own, and spending time inside them. These activities, and the skills that they involve, help children see themselves as strong, capable, and competent. When children experience themselves this way, their confidence makes them more likely to persist in the face of challenges and to engage deeply with materials and ideas.

In the kitty house story, the outdoors supported persistence by offering each child materials and space to explore and express a variety of ideas. Lucas spent many days collecting "straight sticks with no pokey things on them," to use to build the roof and walls. Amelia discovered some paving stones that she decided would make a "perfect kitty house entrance" where they could wipe their paws. Lucas and Amelia worked together to create a "trap door" for the kitties to use as a back entrance. They also experimented with "sharpening their claws" on a variety of surfaces, including tree trunks and fallen logs. All of the children spent time inside the kitty house, imagining, acting out, and talking about how it is to be a real, live kitty.

The wide range of ways these children engaged in "being kitties" shows their deep involvement with applying their ideas to new situations. They built their home. They scavenged for food. They pretended to be a family. They made repairs. Their teacher understood and valued their interest and was instrumental in supporting their engagement. She helped them find materials. She asked questions and monitored and helped them test the safety of their structure. She encouraged them to bring out paper, markers, and string when they wanted to make signs for their house. She created classroom discussion time for the children when issues came up that needed to be discussed in the group. These are all examples of ways teachers support and extend children's engagement with longer-term projects that, even with very young children, may persist over weeks and months.

Choose one of the two stories described, Potato Story or Kitty House. Create a web that records the many different skills and activities children initiated along the way. What further extensions can you suggest?

INDICATOR 3: *The child continues to attempt a difficult task, sustaining attention and working through attendant frustration, disappointment, difficulties, and obstacles.*

WORM STORY

"Look! There are worms!"

What looks like idle scuffing of the bark mulch with their feet as they sit together on the wall is in fact two boys looking for earthworms. They are purposeful as they dig through the bark mulch into the soil below. When one of the boys finds a worm, he gently extracts it from the soil, places it carefully on his palm to show his friend, then offers to find one for his friend as well.

"I found a worm in the dirt. I am going to find you one." The friend declines the offer: "I am finding my own worm." They continue to work and talk, discussing where to find the best worms, and considering what kinds of spaces on their play yard are "favorite" worm spots.

"The worms are probably down in the bottom cause they like dirt."

"I can't find them. . . ."

"I found one. It made a loop de loop. There."

A third child, Rahim, new to the center and not yet fluent in English, has been watching them intently. He approaches them, trying to get a closer look at the worm in one boy's hands. Standing between the two, he shows his interest in joining their work by looking enthusiastically at the worm. The two boys ignore his overtures and go back to their searching. Rahim leaves their area and moves farther away. He begins an investigation of his own, digging with his feet and examining the moist soil under the mulch. After digging for a few moments, he approaches the two boys again and energetically communicates to them that there is better worming to be had farther down the bench. He points to a spot and emphatically states, "There are worms!" When one boy looks interested, he states it again. This time both boys look. Beckoning them to follow him, he runs over to the new spot.

THE OUTDOORS has a generous supply of interesting objects and phenomena that offer children opportunities to engage with materials and with each other. A rich outdoor setting has an almost endless variety and number of things to be discovered and explored. A well-provisioned classroom might have thirty natural objects in the science corner, but outside the number of objects available for investigation is too big to count, each one different from the others. In outdoor settings, children are constantly making discoveries they are eager to share. This is enormous motivation for communication. Their excitement and interest act as fuel for social interaction—they are naturally eager to talk about what they are seeing, feeling, discovering, and wondering about. Such discoveries carry power, creating the potential for all children to find a way to make a social connection if they want to. Even when they encounter strong resistance from other children, such as Rahim experiences, strategies for the persistent child are more available in the outdoors where there are so many opportunities for shared interest and engagement.

It can be hard for children to make new friends, especially if they come midyear into the group and are not fluent in the dominant language. This story illustrates how the outdoor environment provides tools and resources to help children with this difficult task of making connections. Rahim was able to observe and analyze the activity of the other two boys from a comfortable distance. When he tried to join their activity and was unsuccessful, he moved away but did not give up. Instead, he mirrored their activity, digging for worms on his own, and made some of his own discoveries. Equipped with this new experience and his motivation, he had the confidence to approach them again and try to join their play. This time, he offered to share his special worm place as another strategy for building a connection with them.

BALANCING ACT

"I like to practice."

Devin bounds from one stump to the next as he chooses his own pathway from one end of the arrangement of stumps to the other. Moving continuously, he extends his arms as he balances, traveling in a fluid motion, not pausing between his steps. Stepping from a large stump to a much smaller one, he stumbles and jumps to the ground. He stops, studies the two stumps, and climbs back up. He continues forward, now looking down at his feet as he places them. He walks the course two more times, falling only once. After five minutes or so, he jumps to the open ground in the middle of the stumps. Stretching out on the ground, he slithers on his belly like a snake on the mulch. Suddenly, he coils himself up and leaps back to his feet, climbs onto a stump, and resumes his travel from one end of the course to the other.

CHILDREN NEED OPPORTUNITIES to move and to develop their motor planning, balance, strength, and stamina. Climbing, jumping, running, hopping, and other rapid movements are all necessary activities for children's healthy growth and development, though they are generally not safe in the confines of a busy indoor classroom. However, such activities can be readily accommodated in open spaces outdoors. The outdoors provides both planned and unplanned physical challenges for children. Walking in the woods, children need to negotiate varied terrain, step over obstacles, and be alert to their surroundings. In the same way, nonstandardized play structures, such as an irregularly spaced collection of securely anchored stumps of different heights and sizes, require children to engage closely. They must pay attention to where they place their feet and notice where their body is in space. Physical challenges like these encourage persistence. To achieve mastery, children must practice and overcome periodic frustration and disappointment by initiating the challenging activity over and over again.

As his words illustrate, Devin understood the relationship between practice and mastery. He was enjoying the process of perfecting his skillful performance on the stump course. He was also managing his own frustration when he made an error, absorbed the lesson, and moved forward. Knowledge of results is a powerful motivator. When children recognize themselves getting better at a task, it fuels their determination to work harder to reach the goal they have set for themselves. Knowledge of results also helps them manage their frustrations when they confront an obstacle or setback. Physical challenges are especially exciting and engaging for children. Because of this, children apply themselves with great discipline to their goals. The persistence children demonstrate with physical tasks transfers to their efforts in other realms as they both practice and generalize an ability to stay with a difficult task. Like Devin, children who believe that they will be able to achieve a good result tend to demonstrate "stick-to-itiveness" in all aspects of their learning.

In both Worm Story and Balancing Act, the teacher chose not to intervene and to allow the child to work through the challenge he was experiencing on his own. What is the evidence that this was a reasonable and appropriate decision on the part of the teacher?

INDICATOR 4: *The child purposefully chooses activities and interactions of interest, develops a plan, and follows through with increasing independence.*

SNOW SCALE

"I'm making a machine. It's my latest invention. You cover it with snow and then you cover it with a board. Then it turns the snow to ice. This one [board] is perfect! Now more snow and another block. I push this forward and put another block in front."

After twenty minutes of exploring the snow, most of the children go inside with one of their teachers, but Kiri chooses to stay outside. She is trying to pack the fluffy snow into a small snow person. After adding a single eye to her six-inch-tall snow figure, she stops, looks around and moves to the outdoor blocks area. Using her slippery-mittened hands, she tugs a board from the pile, lays it on the ground, and begins shoveling snow over the whole length of the board with her hands. When the board is fairly well covered, she gets another board and places it on top of the first. When she notices that it is not the same width, she rejects it. She returns to the storage area and comes back with one that is the same width, which she places neatly on top of the first. Using the weight of her hand, she cements the two boards together with the snow in between. She then piles snow on each end of the board, brings two big blocks, and cements each one down in the same way. She uses the end of her mitten to smooth the edges neatly, like the bead of caulking around a bathtub. At this point, her focus changes. Putting a crosspiece with blocks at each end she proclaims, "It's like a little scale. It measures things."

THE CHANGES that weather brings to the outdoors are vivid and interesting to young children. Some of these changes, like freshly fallen snow, allow children to experience their outdoor play space in new ways, adding the unfamiliar to the familiar. Children need time to notice changes like wind, shadows, and rain so they can experience the weather and its effects firsthand. To do this, they need more time and space than most early childhood programs provide. And for this they also need the right clothing. Kiri was comfortable working outdoors in the cold for more than an hour because she was staying warm and dry. She had good winter boots, a jacket, a hat, and mittens. She also had a backup set of clothes in her cubby in case she needed them.

Children thrive when they have multiple opportunities to be outside each day. To really engage in issues that interest them requires a good, fat hour of uninterrupted time outside. When children are given generous stretches of time, they are more able to engage and settle in to their activities. Over time and with repeated experience, children develop more complex projects for themselves and richer interactions with one another. They tend to persist longer at a task and with greater focus and engagement.

Kiri was involved with big questions. Although she may not have had the vocabulary to name it, the project she designed for herself was about simple machines and involved the scientific process. She discovered an interest in how the snow behaves and from that interest developed a plan. She decided to invent a machine that "turns snow to ice." The design of her machine incorporated what she had learned about the snow when she was packing it with her hands. By compressing the snow, first with her hands, then between two boards, and finally between the board and a block, she was able to explore her interest—how to change the snow into ice. This story illustrates how engagement grows out of interaction over time. When children pursue questions of deep interest to them, and are given the expanse of time they need to do so, their engagement, their follow through, and their persistence are all enhanced. With such important and interesting questions to explore, it was not surprising that Kiri remained focused on her invention for an hour, bundled up and happily enjoying the winter weather.

LAUNCHING PAD

"Hey! I got an idea!"

Aaron, Connor, and Mason are taking turns leaping from a low platform that they are building with outdoor unit blocks. They are using the storage box for the blocks as a base and using the lid as a launching pad. After each jump, they talk together about changes they want to make to their design. Aaron first supports the launching pad with just one block, placing it vertically in the middle of the front edge of the lid. After he leaps successfully from this structure, Mason suggests that it will be stronger if they add another block. The boys then experiment with the placement of the second block. They first try it at the back, next to the storage box, then move it to the front, adjusting the other block so that each one supports one of the front corners of the lid.

CHILDREN ARE ACTIVE LEARNERS. This means they learn by doing, and learning by doing inevitably involves some level of risk. It is particularly important to understand and plan for the role of risk taking in children's growth and development in the outdoors where children are more active and necessarily make more decisions on their own. Teachers need to design both outdoor spaces and protocols to be responsible and responsive to support children as they test their strengths and confront their limitations. Risk taking involves children in trial and error as a mode of learning and often leads to innovative and creative problem solving. When they succeed, it builds their self-esteem. When they fail, they learn to acknowledge their boundaries and limitations, develop judgment, and deal with the negative emotions that accompany failure. You help children by forming a partnership with them and engaging in conversations that identify and assess risks. This is an important way to help children develop an understanding of what constitutes a reasonable risk. It is one of the ways you help keep children safe.

Aaron, Connor, and Mason chose an activity that was rich in learning partly because it involved a level of risk that was just right for them; it enabled these boys to challenge themselves and experience their physical competence. The engagement showed on their faces as they spent more than thirty minutes tinkering with the balance of their platform and leaping into space. When children are given the opportunity to choose something of deep personal interest and pursue it at a high level, their stake in the activity and its outcome is great. This is the powerful link between persistence and choice. Persistence is a habit that can be cultivated by giving children the opportunity to be deeply involved in projects and pursuits that captivate their imaginations and support each child's sense of self. As persistence develops, it becomes an attitude that can be consciously harnessed and applied to all aspects of children's learning. This will stand them in good stead in later life when they must complete tasks in which they are not as inherently interested.

In both of these stories, Snow Scale and Launching Pad, a set of outdoor wooden blocks is instrumental in the children's activities. What materials on your play yard offer similar open-ended opportunities for children to design and carry out their own projects and explorations?

INDICATOR 5: *The child seeks and accepts help, information, tools, and materials from peers and adults when needed.*

GARDEN DAY

"That's right . . . just keep loosening those roots so they can grow."

It is the annual school community garden day. Grandparents, parents, siblings, and the preschool children are all busy digging and planting together on the play yard. Keisha looks over the various flats and pots of vegetables and flowers her teacher has set out for planting. Pulling on a pair of garden gloves to keep her hands clean, she walks over to the collection of brightly colored annual flowers. She selects a number of plants to put into one of the empty raised beds. After arranging them on top of the soil, Keisha follows her mother's suggestion to knock the Sweet Williams gently out of their pots by tapping the bottoms and turning them upside down. Seeing that the roots are tangled and dry, her mother proposes that she tease them apart with her fingers so that they will be ready to grow in the soil, "That's right . . . just keep loosening those roots so they can grow."

WHILE CHILDREN can learn a great deal from starting seeds in indoor pots and watching them grow, garden experiences outdoors hold opportunities for children that cannot be duplicated inside. Outdoors, children can grow many more kinds of plants and engage with their whole bodies. They can be affected by the weather and other elements of the larger natural world such as insects, birds, falling leaves, and passing clouds. They can actually harvest flowers and herbs, and grow food that they can eat. Good pick-and-eat crops include radishes, carrots, sugar snap peas, cherry tomatoes, lettuce, and other greens. Fun to plant and easier for small hands to manage are garlic, potatoes, spring onions, melons, squash, okra, and sunflowers. Exciting crops to harvest in the late summer and fall include watermelons, pumpkins, and other gourds. Participating throughout the growing season allows children to begin to understand what plants need to grow and thrive, as well as where their food actually comes from, a concept increasingly removed from most children's experience.

Asking for and receiving help with complex and challenging tasks is an important step for children on their way to independence. For this strategy to work well for children, it is important to respond respectfully with just the right amount of help. Often you have to break down the child's question or the task into manageable parts that they can accomplish independently. To accomplish this, you should observe and have conversations with the children that enable you to know what the children are thinking. In this example, the question for the educator is how much help is too much?

Welcoming children's questions and requests for help, engaging them in conversation, and observing and collaborating with them allows adults to find ways to support children. It is important to do this without taking over a task and doing too much, or alternatively, letting them flounder by offering too little. By observing her carefully and working beside her, Keisha's mom was able to see exactly how much and what kind of help to provide so Keisha could do as much of the planting as she was ready to do on her own.

Asking for and providing help are usually not thought of as steps toward independence. But this story shows that providing help allowed a child to complete the task she had set out for herself as independently as possible at the time. Keisha's mother was helping her by providing just the right level and amount of assistance, and no more. When adults respond in this way, children are comfortable seeking the help they need. The result is that they continue to stretch themselves to engage in increasingly difficult tasks.

WATER PUMP

"You gotta push the button!"

Ava and Keisha are playing together in the sand. They are digging a wide hole and lining it with round stones. They then decide to fill their hole with

water. Ava grabs a tall, thin, aqua-colored bucket and runs to the pump. She places the bucket upright in the sand under the outlet for the pump where she predicts the water will pour out. She goes to the back of the pump to push the stainless steel button that controls the flow of water. Each time she pushes the button, the force of the spurt of water hitting the side of the bucket knocks it over. The water spills out into the sand. Shouting her frustration, she recruits Keisha to come and help. Ava squats down and holds the bucket steady while Keisha pushes the button to fill it with water. The two girls smile, return to the sand, and pour the water into their small pond.

You design activities to encourage independence. You also value children's ability to collaborate with others. When collaboration rather than independence is the goal, how can your choice of materials and the arrangement of the outdoor space encourage this?

THE OUTDOORS enables children to experiment with messy materials like sand and water without the constraints of having to be quiet, tidy, and neat. This means that ideas can flow more freely and children can experiment in ways they might not be able to inside where they and their teachers have to be more concerned about cleanup and noise. The outdoor sandbox, for example, naturally inspires exploration of the big ideas of physics such as gravity, force, flow, and erosion. Paired with a water source, the sand area offers an endless stream of learning experiences for children that are unavailable indoors and that often lead to groups of children engaging together in projects lasting for hours, and sometimes days and weeks.

Even though experience taught her that this particular water pump works most easily with two people helping each other, Ava attempted using it a number of different ways by herself. Ava is a child who does not easily ask for help from peers or adults. Had she not been so motivated to fill the pond she had built, she might have given up and found something else to do. Instead, she persisted, enlisting Keisha to come and help. In the outdoors, where children stretch themselves to solve real problems of their own design, they often bump up against tasks that require help or collaboration from a peer. Children like Ava who are hesitant to ask for help from a classmate are more likely to be able to ask for and accept the help they need when they are deeply committed to a project. The increased flexibility Ava showed in accepting help is an example of how highly motivating activities engender persistence. Meaningful projects encourage children to connect with others and to ask for, accept, and give help. All these behaviors allow them to extend their ideas and work in more complex ways.

Further Reflection

How might applying the engagement and persistence standard affect your teaching outdoors?

Different from curiosity, which is inborn, engagement and persistence are functions of children's experience. The fact that engagement and persistence arise from experience puts a greater burden on teachers to attend to and plan for the development of these learning habits. The stories in this chapter all illustrate the effect of children's interest and engagement on their ability to be persistent.

Potato Story and Kitty House, in particular, show how long-term projects can function as both a means and the measure of children's development of this standard. When children have an opportunity to return to materials and ideas day after day and over weeks and months, they think more broadly and deeply about the ideas they are involved with. They bring more of themselves to the task and use materials in innovative ways. They take appropriate risks and behave in more independent ways. The outdoors is particularly well suited to children's involvement in long-term projects. It provides a wealth of open-ended materials that inspire children to find expression and to experiment with their ideas. In addition, children can usually initiate, pursue, leave, and come back to projects outside without having to dismantle them at the end of the day. When children are captivated by long-term projects, they are demonstrating their engagement and developing their persistence.

Most outdoor activities have multiple entry points allowing children to become engaged in many different ways. The outdoors is a setting having "room for everyone." By carefully structuring time, space, and materials, you can nurture children's interests and commitment to tasks that are "just right" for each child. When children choose to stay with a project, they have the opportunity to form the deeper engagement that is linked to persistence.

To invent, you need a good imagination and a pile of junk.
THOMAS EDISON

Imagination, Invention, and Creativity Standard

IMAGINATION, INVENTION, AND CREATIVITY are the language of early childhood. The world is new to children, filled with mysteries for them to experience and try to understand. To do this, they have to put unknown things together in "new" ways and observe, sort, and begin to classify the elements of their experience. Invention is, in a sense, the only option when you don't know exactly how things work or what to expect. It is through invention, creativity, and the imagination that children can play with what they are seeing and experiencing, and look at it from different angles to form an understanding. Whether they are painting, role playing, building a structure, dancing, or telling a story, children have to sort through, test, and reimagine their experience over and over again.

As necessary as they are, imagination, invention, and creativity are increasingly less valued in early childhood programs and schools. They are also rarely understood to be the important learning tools that they are. For children, they are essential ways of coming to know the world, and therefore, powerful approaches to learning. Teachers know that the creative process is actually a way of knowing. The child who pretends to be a mother bird sitting on her nest, warming her eggs, and watching out for danger is finding a way to apply what she has seen and heard about birds. She is refining her understanding about them and their behavior. The child who builds a bridge with blocks over an imaginary river is exploring concepts like over and under, up and down, as well as confronting the physics of engineering.

Overview

Why is the imagination, invention, and creativity standard important for healthy child development?

Imagination is possibly the most powerful tool people have. It allows you to sit in a chair in your living room and travel through time and space without moving an inch. People learn by doing and by imagining. Imagining enables you to put things together in new ways, form new associations and connections, and come to new understandings. When a person asks, "What if?" a door opens to fresh possibilities, solutions, and ideas. Asking "What if I were the new baby?" allows a child to explore and experience through role play what that coming change in the family may be like. Asking "What if I put this blue paint with the yellow?" enables a child to invent the color green. Asking "What if I were a fairy princess?" empowers a child to feel beautiful and important. Asking "What if I use the snow to hold the blocks together?" creates a new solution to a problem. The vehicle of imaginary play provides children with a way to explore the world, solve problems, and develop confidence. Children love to do things "just for pretend" and to process through their play what is real and what is make-believe.

Part of the work of childhood is to develop a healthy sense of self. A child's identity and self-esteem are enhanced through creative self-expression. As children participate in acts of imagination and create new ideas and explore new mediums, they come to know themselves as unique and valuable. Therefore, it is important that teachers provide an environment that encourages children to engage in imaginative play and inventiveness and supports their creative self-expression.

Pragmatic View

How do states and national early childhood organizations classify imagination, invention, and creativity?

Compared to both curiosity and initiative, and engagement and persistence, far fewer states address imagination, invention, and creativity directly in their standards. Were this the only information about these particular approaches to learning, one might think that they are less important than the standards mentioned more frequently. This would be a mistake. Imagination, invention, and creativity are critical capacities that affect all areas of a child's development. Making sense of the world is the work of early childhood; social/imaginative play, with its reliance on invention and creativity, is a primary vehicle available to children for doing this important work. As Vivian Paley writes, "Ideas and purposes must be processed through other children in social play if a child is to open up to an ever larger picture and determine how the pieces fit together" (1988, viii). Children represent the real world through their play and this is how they make sense of it. The ability to engage in imaginative play is also a form of abstract thinking, which relates to children's capacity to succeed in school.

In looking at the states where the early learning standards do directly address imagination, invention, and creativity, a clear theme of self-expression emerges. Standards stress the ability to make independent decisions, see new ways to do things, and try original ways to combine materials. The theme of role play and fantasy play as exploratory tools for children also emerges. Lastly, a few states recognize the importance of humor as an indicator of a child's capacity for self-expression and creativity.

Applied View

What are the observable behaviors or indicators that demonstrate children engaging with the imagination, invention, and creativity standard?

This standard, although critically important to children's development, is less frequently mentioned by states across the country than others that appear in this book. This indicates to us not that it is less important, but rather that it is less well understood and perhaps harder for teachers to quantify and systematically teach. Yet, it is essential for making sense of the world and vitally important in the learning process. It is the predisposition that fuels new ideas, discoveries, innovation, experimentation, problem solving, and creative expression. Imagination is necessary for hypothesis formation and therefore scientific discovery.

Some aspects of imagination are recognized by states. The use of materials in new and original ways appears in numerous states as a marker for creativity and invention and is, by definition, a clear sign of this standard. Pretend play is another common strong thread running through these standards. A third indicator, humor, appears and is a more sophisticated marker. It shows the child's ability to juxtapose contradictory ideas and play with the tension that creates. When children use humor appropriately and creatively to express an idea, it is a sign that they have made a connection and that they understand something new.

We have synthesized the observable behaviors articulated in the various state standards for imagination, invention, and creativity for three- to five-year-old children into the following three indicators:

1. The child exhibits, appreciates, and enjoys a sense of humor.

2. The child engages in pretend play, expressing feelings, trying out new ideas and behaviors, and role playing using real or make-believe objects.

3. The child explores and experiments, trying new ways of doing things by combining and using materials in novel and original ways.

Experiencing the Imagination, Invention, and Creativity Standard in the Outdoors

INDICATOR 1: *The child exhibits, appreciates, and enjoys a sense of humor.*

THE TRAIN

"Which track do you want to go on?"
  "Let's go to the North Pole . . . to see basketball!"
  "Are you the motor? . . . cause only the motor can be in the back of the train."

Cole and Sebastian are following each other, balancing on a flat timber that surrounds one of the play areas on their play yard. Moving fast, they occasionally throw out an arm to maintain their balance. They call to a third boy, "Do you want to get on the train, Aaron?" Aaron jumps up behind them and says, "I'm the motor," and the three boys take off in rhythm. They all make train noises and move their arms like pistons as they navigate the "track." They glance at each other and giggle as they turn the corner. When they come to an intersection where the timbers go in two different directions, Cole, who is at the front, asks the others which way they want to go. Sebastian, who is in the middle, volunteers that they should go to the North Pole, pauses for a moment and then adds with a big smile, " . . . to see basketball!" They all laugh as they turn left and proceed down the track.

THE OUTDOORS provides a welcoming space for the big energy, boisterous activity, and loud voices that are a part of the natural expression of young children. Many children, boys in particular, find themselves in school situations where their exuberance and physicality are not easily accommodated. The outdoors has the capacity to absorb this creative energy. Children often display more laughter and humor when they are outside. Outdoor environments support extended pretend play and fantasy and the bigger movements of running, jumping, climbing, and skipping. These are all modes through which children can express and enjoy their developing relationship with humor.

Much of children's humor during their preschool years is expressed through physical energy, by doing things as well as talking about them. There are many opportunities for humor in children's social interactions and play. For example, "backwards day" is terribly funny to four-year-old children because it is all about doing exactly the opposite of what they know to be correct or expected. The humor springs from their growing understanding of the world around them and their new ability to see or create discontinuities or contradictions.

In the story above, Cole, Sebastian, and Aaron were sharing an extended joke. They were playing with ideas, using both words and the actions of their bodies. What's funny about being a train? One thing is that trains make funny sounds and it is humorous to mimic them. The three boys traveled the "track," all in synchronized movement, chugging along past their friends, making sounds, and rotating their arms in unison like pistons. As it is in classic slapstick humor, part of the fun was in the exaggerated movements they were making. They were perfectly in sync, sharing the same rhythm with precise timing and execution. Added to the silliness involved in being a train was the verbal joke the boys shared about their destination. They chose a most unlikely place for a train to take them, and then paired it with basketball, a most unlikely activity to find at the North Pole. Their quick and easy laughter when Sebastian suggested basketball at the North Pole demonstrated that they were all sharing and understanding the joke.

CLIMBING THE GULLY

"Hold on! We'll pull you up!"

The four-year-old children are playing in the woods. They are experimenting with climbing the steep side of the small gully. It is hard to do, and they frequently fall back down before they reach the top. Lucas, Zoe, and Molly decide to use two three-foot-long foam noodles from the play yard to pull one another up. First they do it with one puller and one climber. They practice diligently until they can pull each other up with confidence. Then, they begin to play with taking turns being one of two pullers, or being the climber. Each time they try to pull a person up, someone "unexpectedly" lets go, either the climber or one of the pullers, and the climber rolls down to the bottom over the soft earth. When this happens, all three children collapse into giggles, saying "Let's try it again!" or "Let's try it this way!"

THE OUTDOORS offers unique and intriguing physical challenges, like those posed by the topography of the gully. In this story, the children and the hill are a perfect unit in which the children respond to the pull of gravity, the inclined plane, and the uneven surface that the gully provides. Its structure enables the children to stage their own learning. They take on the challenge of hill climbing in steps that make sense to them. First they explore the hillside, choosing more and less steep ways to go up, and they practice rolling down to test the steepness of the hill from a different point of view. After a period of hands-on exploration, they develop the skills and confidence that come from setting and meeting a series of increasingly complex goals. Their trust, both in their own skills and in one another, enables them to begin to play with the ideas and concepts behind their work. The resulting humor is actually a clear and useful indication of their mastery of the physical and conceptual challenges the gully offers.

This story is about a pretend game in which everyone understood and was playing with the same set of rules. The rules were clear. You pretended to try your best to climb up the hill if you were the climber. You pretended to try your best to pull if you were a puller. But, whether you were a climber or a puller, the joke was that your goal was really to have the climber roll back down the hill rather than get to the top. The game required improvisation, timing, and judgment. It also involved trust and confidence, which the children developed together at the beginning of their play when they were learning to climb the hill together. The humor followed this initial mastery, and came from the discontinuity between what seemed to be the expectation and what was really going on. Once the children practiced and could actually climb the hill, then they could play with the idea of not being able to climb the hill and find it funny. A great deal of theatrics went into the falls with exaggerated rolling, tumbling, slow-motion movement, expressions of surprise— all amid great laughter. Lucas, Zoe, and Molly did this over and over for thirty minutes, celebrating their mastery, still laughing as hard at the end as when they started the game.

Valuing children's humor can help you understand what they are thinking about and feeling and where they are developmentally. What are the characteristics of young children's humor that you enjoy? What aspects of their humor are hard for you to engage with?

INDICATOR 2: *The child engages in pretend play, expressing feelings, trying out new ideas and behaviors, and role playing using real or make-believe objects.*

THE SPACESHIP

"It's a blaster. You push this special button. First, you have to pull this down. It's the gasser. It gives a lot of energy. Then, you push the button. Then, you have the countdown and you blast off . . . 5 . . . 4 . . . 3 . . . 2 . . . 1 . . . 0 . . . BLAST OFF!"

It is a drizzly day in the fall. The children and their teacher put on raincoats and rain boots and go outside puddle jumping. From the puddles in the gravel, they move into the woods to look for colorful leaves. Once there, some of the children notice the root-ball of a fallen tree. Jacob exclaims, "Look, a spaceship!" They climb up and claim the top of the ball as a control room, using the saplings surrounding the space as controls and levers to operate the ship. After a few minutes of play, Molly climbs down and walks to a large stump fifteen feet away, where she reenacts the blast-off countdowns many times by herself. For over twenty minutes she practices and refines her system, designating special buttons, parts, and functions for the stump.

IN THE NATURAL WORLD, the sky is the limit in terms of the number of different ways children can decide to use the settings and loose parts they find there. The root-ball of the fallen tree serves these children as a spaceship in this story. It could serve equally well as a cabin, a castle, a fairy house, or a school bus. The materials of nature are flexible and ambiguous. This quality allows children to read their own meaning into them. The ambiguity of the materials makes them ideal prompts for children's imagination, fitting easily into the stories children create for themselves in their play. Leaves become money or medicine or fairy blankets; sticks are magic wands or writing pens; moss might be a fuzzy animal. When children are outside, they rarely lack the props they need to pursue a new creative idea.

When adults go out in the rain, they often do so hesitantly. They tend to cringe a bit, shut down their senses, and look down at the ground instead of out at the world. When the weather is wet, cold, or particularly hot, they often try to stay outside for as short a period of time as possible. In general, children do not naturally respond this way. The children in this story are clearly experiencing wet weather in a different way. They had been jumping in puddles, noticing the vibrant color in the wet fall leaves, and exploring the transformation of the dirt into soft, wet mud. As far as they were concerned, it was a deeply interesting day outside and many of them were eager to stay outside as long as possible. Why is this?

Children are naturally interested in experiencing changes in the weather and in investigating how those changes affect their environment. The teacher working with these children values the changes in the weather as important learning opportunities. Investigating weather and its effects is a critical activity for children and is necessary for them to develop a more complete picture of their world. Therefore, their teacher wants them to have varied and intriguing experiences outside. She plans for those experiences, making sure that parents send children with the right clothing to keep them warm and dry, no matter the weather. By going outside every day, she gives the children access to multiple worlds. They come to know and appreciate the wet and rainy day, the cold day, the foggy day, the snowy day. Each day is unique and exciting and brings its own set of experiences to their imaginative play.

THE BAKERY

"That's such a beautiful cake. You spent a lot of time on that. We'll have to leave it out for the birdies."

Many of the children have been playing bakery, using dishes and utensils in the outdoor playhouse and the sandbox. Using the sand, they measure, stir, and pour ingredients into cake pans. Liam fills a cake pan to the brim and smoothes out the surface, saying, "Pat, pat, pat. Pat it down." He sets the pan down on a wooden bench and walks over to the shrubs growing along the fence. He kneels down on the ground and quietly gathers several leaves of different colors, some twigs, and some brown seeds. He takes these items back and carefully arranges them on top of his cake. Just as he finishes decorating it, the teacher announces it is time to clean up and put everything away. She notices Liam holding his cake and looking upset. Rather than directing him to pour out the

sand and put the pan back in the bin, she compliments his careful work and suggests that they leave this lovely cake out for the birds to eat. "That's such a beautiful cake. You spent a lot of time on that. We'll have to leave it out for the birdies."

ALMOST EVERY DAY in preschool someone is celebrating a real or imaginary birthday or creating a special pretend food or snack of some kind. Eating and feeding others "just for pretend" starts with very young children, who mime this activity with their caregivers. This kind of imaginary creative play springs from children's familiarity with the rituals of daily life, experiences they share with others, first with their family, then with peers and teachers. Children reenact these rituals and activities, particularly around food and eating, because they are familiar, important, and pleasurable. It is eminently satisfying to children to create a cake or pie, or put a meal on the table. Sharing "food" in this way enables children to think about issues of connectedness.

These activities work particularly well outside where children can forage. They can look for and find special ingredients, decorations, or condiments by combing the sand where the acorns fall or carefully selecting fragrant leaves from the wax myrtle. Pretend play involves many skills: problem solving, aesthetic judgment, role playing, small-motor skills, and conversation. Through such play, children come to know their outdoor spaces intimately, noticing small changes over the course of the year, recognizing particular shapes and smells of trees and flowers, and feeling at home in this special world.

Liam was focused and engaged, making careful choices as he decorated his cake. He was completely absorbed in the process and he was having fun. The call for cleanup came as an unhappy surprise. He was upset at the prospect of having to abandon his project and dump out his work. His observant teacher noticed his distress right away and, further, understood why he was feeling so unhappy. In response to her observations, she was able to think flexibly about the direction she gave the children to put everything away and devised a solution that she thought might feel better to Liam. She suggested to him that rather than dump out his beautiful cake, he offer to share it with the birds. This is an example of the kind of difficult judgment calls teachers must make all day long. They must weigh many priorities related to scheduling, curriculum, materials, and management while also respecting children's needs and sensibilities. The educator in this story was both observant and flexible. She was able to stretch her own understanding of "clean up" to accommodate Liam's need to save his work.

What makes imaginary play such a critical component of children's early development? How do you support imaginary play outdoors?

INDICATOR 3: *The child explores and experiments, trying new ways of doing things by combining and using materials in novel and original ways.*

THE SHARK

"I'm going to turn this shark into a pussycat."

Tarik has been working at the outdoor sand table digging in the dark red sand. He fills measuring cups, scooping the sand with spoons, then pouring it out over plastic animals and sea creatures to "bury" them. Choosing a shark from the array of animals at the table, he looks closely at it, turning it in his hands to observe its wide, gaping mouth, its sharp needlelike teeth, and its curving tail. After studying it, he takes the shark to the nearby deck where paint, brushes, and water are all available. Dipping a long brush into the bright red paint and brushing it carefully onto the shark's side, Tarik firmly states that he is going to "turn this shark into a pussycat."

NATURE models for children the possibilities inherent in new combinations, offering examples of transformation for them to notice. The yellow leaf that lands in the pond creates unexpected reflections. The acorn that seats itself in the planter sprouts a volunteer oak tree. Sand blows across the path and changes its texture. Ice forms on the surface of the bird bath. When children themselves are allowed to combine materials or move them from one center to another, they naturally discover new possibilities and ideas. The outdoors lends itself to this movement of objects and ideas from place to place, a mixing process that supports creativity. By carrying the shark from the sand table to the paint area, Tarik was reorganizing and combining elements in his environment in an original way and from this came a new idea. With the paint, he was able to transform the shark into anything he could imagine. Such creative and dramatic transformations are more likely to occur in settings where children are allowed to explore, recombine, and reimagine the elements of their world.

This story illustrates how adults often see the spaces children use differently from how children themselves experience those spaces. Teachers plan and equip spaces or centers, both indoors and out, with certain kinds of activities or engagements in mind. They arrange the outdoor sand table for digging, pouring, burying, and rediscovering things, and creating stories or interactions with toys or other objects. Tarik's story illustrates that children understand their spaces in a more fluid way. They often want to take an idea and run with it. Tarik had the opportunity to follow the idea he had of transforming the shark from the sand table over to the area where there were materials that would help him do so. Tarik did not draw a line between work he did at the sand table and work he could do in the paint area. His teacher encouraged children to follow their ideas over time and through space by moving between and among centers. You support children's drive to invent, create, and imagine when you allow children to combine materials in novel and expressive ways. You can facilitate this by being sure that the children know where to find and where to return the different materials and tools they need.

GARDEN FAIRIES

"If we give it some water, it will give us blueberries for a thank-you."

Fairy costumes are very popular with the girls in this group. On this sunny spring day, they run outside, take the dresses out of the costume box, examine them closely, and help each other choose the prettiest one. They slip the dresses over their shorts and shirts, and fasten them up the back. Some of the girls attach fairy wings to their arms. They then go off to play. Two girls choose to share a tricycle, another girl runs up the hill, and Ava and Sierra fly together over to the sand area. They grab two watering cans and fill them to the brim from the water pump. They then walk so as not to spill, to water the blueberry bushes by the shade shelter.

COSTUMES are useful props that help children take on different roles and play at life from different points of view. Adopting a role or becoming a make-believe character enables children to try on feelings, actions, and responses that may be different from their own. By applying these adopted emotions and behaviors in a variety of settings, children extend their own repertoire of skills and responses. When costumes are restricted to a stage or dress-up area, children's opportunities are confined to what is available in that place. Alternatively, when dress-up is encouraged all through the outdoors, children can relate to all aspects of the here and now through the lens of a different person, using their imaginations to develop ideas and dialogues from this new point of view. Pretend play allows children to combine socially in new and different ways, which leads to new learning. Finding out what it is like to be a fairy taking care of a garden, a mama bird trying to protect her fledglings that have scattered across the grass, or a police officer stopping traffic is a step toward understanding and predicting the actions, motivations, and behaviors of others and oneself. In this story, Ava and Sierra played together, pretending to be fairies. They conversed and smiled as they enacted the roles they had created for themselves. In this context, they enjoyed one another's company even though they were not girls who ordinarily played together. Ava was sometimes impatient with other children and wanted to do things her own way. Sierra was quiet and still learning English. She often played alone. She did not always understand the rules and expectations that other children were playing by and was uncertain about how to ask for help. Having a role like "fairy" that suggested strongly how to act—what to do and what to say—she could relax and enjoy playing with Ava. Playing a role that provided a script also helped Ava practice her social skills and share leadership for the direction the game would take. The girls shared a bond that was reinforced by the fact that they were both dressed for the part.

Pretend roles can provide a powerful context for children to try out relationships with others they may be interested in but are unsure about how to be with. This is one of the ways that children's experiences are transformed and expanded when they are allowed to become someone else. By sharing the same fantasy, children become part of the same group and have to work together to both create and follow the rules of the game. Within the framework of whatever story they are playing out, they find it easier to talk and interact with each other.

What are the organizational structures and procedures you can put in place that allow children to engage in inventive, important, and sometimes messy work, but that make finding materials and cleaning up afterward more manageable?

Further Reflection

How might applying the imagination, invention, and creativity standard affect your teaching outdoors?

This chapter began with a quote from Thomas Edison identifying creativity as a partnership between the imagination and the environment. It is not enough to be smart and curious. To be creative, children need things to think about, manipulate, and engage with. The materials that children have access to, both indoors and out, are an important influence on how their imaginations develop.

Before adults add even one thing to it, the outdoors is already a wonderful learning space. The natural world comes equipped with countless objects and abundant materials that capture the imagination of the child. It is full of loose parts that children can discover and manipulate, including stones, leaves, seedpods, flowers, twigs, pinecones, and stems. Children are inspired by these loose parts to figure out what they can do with them. Creativity is cultivated when children explore and experiment and try out different ways of doing things with materials.

The materials that nature provides are flexible and open-ended and can be fit together in a myriad of ways according to the inclinations and inventiveness of the child. With so many prompts for the imagination already in place, teachers must observe and think carefully about the specific things to add to further enrich what is already going on. Whether buckets and shovels, magnifying lenses and guide books, big blocks, costumes, or paint and brushes—all will depend on your assessment of just what it is that the children need each day to pursue their work and play outside.

In addition to the things that children can touch and interact with, there are always other fascinating things to watch and wonder about outside: the ongoing show of clouds crossing the sky casting unexpected shadows, the birds flitting from branch to branch, the inchworm hanging from its silken thread that suddenly appears before your eyes, the drama of the spider web with its captured prey. There are so many things to see, many of which come with stories to wonder about. For example, "Where did the ant go when it went under that rock? What is it doing there? Will it come back? Does it have a family? What does it eat?" "What is that bird doing with that twig in its beak? Why does it keep going back and forth between the shrub and that tree?" "Why is there a puddle in the middle of the path after the rain?" Outside, such stories are ever ongoing. They provide an added dimension and a place for each child's own stories, pretend play, make-believe, role play, and creative inventions to unfold.

Too often we give children answers to remember rather than problems to solve.
ROGER LEWIS

Reasoning and Problem-Solving Standard

REASONING AND PROBLEM SOLVING are highly valued learning behaviors in western society and early childhood curricula. Many manufactured materials, such as Cuisenaire rods and attribute blocks, are made specifically to teach reasoning and problem solving in early childhood classrooms. Teachers may be more familiar with reasoning and problem solving than some of the other standards because they are addressed so thoroughly by formal curricula.

But the focus on specific materials can distract teachers from realizing that problem solving is the natural mode of children. In fact, children are engaged with aspects of problem solving all the time. Every moment of their day, children are occupied with trying to figure things out by applying various problem-solving skills and strategies. Knowing this about children, you can enhance their learning by providing them with open-ended materials and the time to explore the materials.

Long periods of uninterrupted time provide children with the opportunity to engage in in-depth exploration and talk with others as they process what they are doing. Ample time, open-ended materials, and dialogue are essential conditions for this standard to be addressed effectively. The natural world provides prime opportunities for these conditions to be met. Therefore, scheduling ample time outdoors gives children access to the ideal setting for pursuing their reasoning and problem-solving skills.

Overview

Why is the reasoning and problem-solving standard important for healthy child development?

Problem solving is at the core of human experience. It is the foundation for all learning. It is the way children make sense of the world and come to understand it, affect it, and control it. As such, problem solving is critical to their development. It is in the early childhood years that children begin to accumulate strategies and tools that they can use to investigate issues, understand how things work, build structures, and work with others. Thinking of all they need to accomplish, it is easy to see how important it is for children to have lots of opportunities to practice and refine their problem-solving skills and strategies. By doing so, they both strengthen the ones they have and develop new ones.

Open-ended projects allow children to try out different strategies, assess the results, make inferences and judgments based on those results, then further refine their approach to the problem. They learn which approach or application is most effective for the type of problem they are trying to solve. They learn that trial and error is not as successful in social situations as collaboration and discussion, but that it is very effective when trying to understand what objects will float on water. They learn that sorting and classifying does not help them understand the behavior of a praying mantis, though it is a great way to learn more about the properties of rocks and minerals. The more strategies or tools children develop and add to their "tool bag," the more possibilities they can draw on as they encounter new issues and questions.

Reasoning is the ability to think critically or analytically about information and experiences. As such it is hard to separate from problem solving, which also involves the application of judgment, logical deduction, and decision making. The two are intertwined, making it difficult to give one priority over the other. They support each other in a spiral of actions as children identify questions, select and apply strategies, evaluate the results, refine the questions, and start again. With each iteration, children increase both the level of their understanding and the skill with which they apply their tools.

Reasoning involves drawing inferences or conclusions from known or assumed facts, whereas problem solving is really an umbrella term for many different processes and strategies. These include trial and error (guessing and checking), dividing and conquering, brainstorming, researching, making analogies, testing hypotheses, looking for patterns, drawing pictures, making models, and asking questions. Identifying these specific actions makes it clear that problem solving thrives in places where children are engaged in active exploration with the opportunity to make choices and decisions themselves. It also thrives when children are really interested in what they are doing.

Pragmatic View

How do states and national early childhood organizations classify reasoning and problem solving?

A number of states include reasoning and problem solving in their early learning standards, listing them either separately or together. The language used to define and describe the behaviors teachers should look for as evidence of reasoning and problem solving often repeats the language of the standard itself. For example, a state may say, "Problem solving is the ability to seek solutions to problems," but the standard neither defines what is meant by problems nor what would be seen if a child were successfully seeking solutions to problems. This makes it difficult for teachers to support children using these standards. What is needed are examples of well-defined behaviors that clearly show the standard in action. The indicators in this chapter provide such examples to support teachers in their observations.

Applied View

What are the observable behaviors or indicators that demonstrate children engaging with the reasoning and problem-solving standard?

In developing a list of indicators for inclusion here, we studied the language, content, and meaning behind state standards and translated them into behavioral terms that teachers can use to observe children as they investigate the world through work and play. The indicators in this chapter address useful strategies or action plans that children apply when reasoning and problem solving effectively. Through practice and experience, children become more skillful and proficient problem solvers as they apply these strategies over time.

When teachers provide environments full of open-ended questions and issues of interest for children to wonder about, they are doing exactly what needs to be done for children to interact with the standard. The outdoors, seen in this context, is a particularly strong partner with the educator because it comes already full of change, mystery, and intensely interesting materials for children to investigate.

The four observable behaviors that follow synthesize the content of the various state standards for both reasoning and problem solving for three- to five-year-olds:

1. The child actively explores the environment and identifies meaningful issues.

2. The child initiates more than one approach or solution in response to questions and dilemmas.

3. The child applies strategies such as trial and error, comparing, sorting, classifying, and organizing to understand and find solutions.

4. The child discusses, consults, and collaborates with other children and adults in working through questions and investigations.

Experiencing the Reasoning and Problem-Solving Standard in the Outdoors

INDICATOR 1: *The child actively explores the environment and identifies meaningful issues.*

ROCK MAN

"I have a lot of rocks in my pocket . . . enough to pull down my pants! I found them over there. I have one black one. Look at this one. It looks like a rectangle. It has three flat sides and the bottom is bumpy. I have a special place in my room where I put all the rocks I find. I used a rock I already had to dig them up. Look at this one! It's pink and orange and green. Look! The hole it was in has green on the outside. Let me see if I can put it back in . . . I don't think I can get it to fit right back in."

Ethan has been digging for rocks for much of the afternoon. He has been collecting his favorites and putting them in his pockets. Suddenly he spies the tip of a piece of rose quartz poking out of the ground. He pries it out gently, using the point of another rock, careful not

to disrupt the hole it came from. Holding the quartz up to the sun, he sees a circle of moss growing all around its middle. He looks back at the hole and notices the same moss around the top edge. Looking back and forth between the rock and the hole, he wonders aloud whether he can replace the rock into its hole and have it be just the way he found it. He squats down and lays the rock on the space it came from, but it will not go back in.

THE ROCK AND THE HOLE were originally a perfect fit and it does not make sense to Ethan that the rock will not slip easily back in where it was before. After all, a wooden puzzle piece can be taken out and then slipped right back in where it was before. But unlike the wooden puzzle, the materials of the natural world are always changing in response to the forces acting on them. By displacing the rock, Ethan disrupts a perfect fit that was formed over time. The rock and the hole can never be reunited as they were before. This provides Ethan with the opportunity to understand that his actions have a direct impact on the environment. The world is different because he is there. What he feels is the same powerful sensation children have when they notice and play with their shadow in the sunlight, or when they deliberately leave their footprints in the mud. In these ways, nature offers children the opportunity to make a mark, to see how the world changes in response to their actions. This is exciting to children, and provides them with important knowledge about the fact that they exist in the world and that they are having an impact on it.

Ethan was deeply engaged in hunting for rocks. As he found them, he examined them carefully and turned them over in his hand. He commented on the details of their color, shape, size, and weight. He sorted them, separating the gray gravel from the stones that had some quartz in them. Periodically, he put some of his favorites into his pocket to take home, explaining that he had a special rock collection on a shelf next to his bed. He said, giggling shyly, "I have so many rocks in my pocket, they are pulling my pants down!" Ethan's fascination with rocks enabled him to begin to see patterns, similarities and differences, and notice things like where the best rocks are found on his play yard and to predict what other rocks he might find in the same place. Focused on the rocks themselves, he stumbled upon an interesting puzzle posed by the rose quartz. He assumed that if he was careful, he could take it out of the ground and then put it back again exactly the way it was before. Investigating this premise further, he discovered this was not so and he wondered why. It will take much more hands-on experience and more time for him to sort out the issues around this interesting question that he is just beginning to explore.

THE CARROT

"Look! It's a carrot from last year. It has a big crack in it!"

The children have just finished eating lunch outside on one of the first warm days of spring. After cleaning up lunch, several of the children begin to collect ground ivy from the raised beds in the vegetable garden. They gather the cupped leaves into bouquets that they give to one another as well as to parents arriving for early pickup. As they work, some of them talk together about the garden. Amelia talks about the carrots they planted and harvested in this bed last year. As she picks the dark, round ivy leaves, she comes upon a light green feathery sprig that is quite different. She picks it and shows it to Carly and Phin, "It's a carrot!" They all begin to search carefully under the leaves for more carrot sprigs. They find several carrot plants that have survived the winter and pull on the delicate foliage. Most of them break off at ground level. But Amelia, pulling carefully, coaxes one small orange carrot out of the ground.

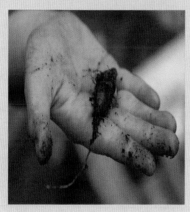

NATURE IS FULL OF THINGS for children to investigate. It is continually changing, providing new things to wonder about and discover. In this story, investigation by the children shows that last year's carrot bed has been overrun with ground ivy. This prompts a question for the children: What happened to the carrots they remember? By following that question, they make a discovery. Underneath the ground cover, some carrot leaves are growing. This discovery triggers yet another new question: Is there a carrot under the ground? This story illustrates how motivating the questions are that children devise for themselves, and how the outdoors, in particular, encourages children to ask and answer questions on their own.

Children are continually confronting interesting events that have come to be without an adult planning them. For example, the garden bed becomes a bed of ground ivy. How did that happen? What does it mean? Are the carrots still there? Where did they go? Such a process of exploring and investigating the environment independently supports children's reasoning and problem-solving skills. This story illustrates how the natural world and its many mysteries encourage this process without a teacher having to plan each piece.

In scheduling your daily routines for young children, what factors argue for long, uninterrupted time outside?

The children in this story were feeling at home outdoors, expressing affection and a sense of ownership for their school yard. Their comfort and familiarity empowered them to investigate and act independently; picking the ground ivy, making bouquets, and giving them to friends and parents. Their teacher had created a structure that supported the children in being responsible and self-sufficient. This environment offered interesting objects, materials, and events for the children to explore. The result was that Amelia, Carly, and Phin could frame and pursue a number of interesting questions springing from their own experiences, interests, and memory of the place. The carrot offered them a gift. It allowed them to connect their memories and understanding of what they did in the garden a year ago to the experience they were having in the garden today.

INDICATOR 2: *The child initiates more than one approach or solution in response to questions and dilemmas.*

SNOWBALL

"It is too fluffy to make snowballs. This is not packing snow. When you throw it, it just falls apart."

Madison does not have a chance to see snow very often in her climate, and is excited by this rare event. There is a lot of snow when she arrives at school and she is eager to get outside and explore it. She scrapes up a big handful of snow from the ground and tries to pack it with her mittened hands. "It is too fluffy to make snowballs. This is not packing snow. When you throw it, it just falls apart." Unable to get it to clump together, she moves to the storage box for the blocks and scoops up the snow on its wooden top. The snow refuses to hold together and she moves again, this time to the wooden timber that surrounds the outdoor sandbox. Lastly she returns to the outdoor block box where the snow is now beginning to melt in the sun. As she scoops the snow at her feet, she says, "Look, here is a different kind of snow." Bending down to investigate, she remarks matter-of-factly, "Look, smell the ground. It has a different smell." Scooping again, she is able to compact the snow enough to form a small snowball. After she packs it as tightly as she can, she tosses it at a wooden post.

SNOW IS AN ABUNDANT and free wintertime educational material in many regions. It offers children the opportunity to dig, pack, sculpt, and explore its unique properties. These properties vary, depending on such factors as the weather, where the snow has fallen, how long ago it fell, whether it has had a chance to melt a bit or freeze, and importantly, what kind of snow it was in the first place. Madison is making distinctions between the qualities of the snow she finds in different locations on the yard. She is acquiring a significant amount of knowledge about snow.

Children are keen observers and take in information with all their senses. Sometimes the details they notice are surprising. Left to their own devices, children are continually comparing and contrasting, asking why, formulating answers, and testing them. Observing children engaged with fascinating materials like snow provides a window into what the children understand and what they are still wondering about.

Madison was highly motivated to make a snowball. She was interested in the problem of how to find snow that would pack and stick together. She knew from her firsthand experience that this particular snow was not good for packing. She also seemed to know that the qualities of snow are ephemeral; they are different in different places and they change over time. This knowledge led her to explore different parts of the yard, testing the snow in each area by trying to pack it together. Her teacher gave her both the time and the space to follow this self-directed investigation independently, allowing her to ask and answer her own questions. By trying a number of different approaches, Madison eventually solved her problem, finding snow that she could pack together into a snowball. Often, adults are tempted to step in and solve such problems for children or offer them unneeded advice. On her own, Madison devised multiple approaches to her dilemma. Her story also illustrates how persistent children can be when they are genuinely interested in the issue they are investigating.

CREEK FLOAT

"Look! It does it! It floats!"

These four-year-old children have a water pump in their sand area. The water empties from the sand into a concrete-lined "creek" that flows under a bridge and out into a small rain garden. Many children are drawn to the water on this hot, early summer day. They drop twigs and leaves into the stream and follow them along as they float under the bridge to the other side. Drawn by the excitement of the children playing by the water, three girls who have been making sand cakes join them, bringing with them fresh green leaves to put in the water. The group of seven children spends the next fifteen minutes experimenting with different natural objects from the play yard to see which ones will float and which ones will sink. As they investigate, they share their observations and questions. Omar, a younger child, watches them. He moves further down the creek to experiment on his own. He collects some grass, twigs, and pods from a redbud tree and drops them one by one in the water, watching intently to see what they do.

A LOT OF children's learning involves what adults might call "just messing about," an open-ended approach to learning that is a characteristic of outdoor play. These children are engaged in a self-directed scientific study that emerges seamlessly—unplanned by their teacher—from their initial interest in touching and being close to the water. Spending time engaged with "simple" activities like floating twigs in water, children learn and explore sophisticated concepts about the behavior of water and the nature of materials.

Exploring in this way involves trying out different ways of doing things and devising different approaches to problems. For example, finding that a pebble does not float, a child might experiment, putting it on top of something that does, alternately trying bark, pine needles, or a large leaf. Or a child might spend ten minutes floating a leaf by itself, watching carefully to see if it goes fast or slow, where the current takes it, and where it ends up. This kind of play is endlessly fun and fascinating. Furthermore, it is essential to children's growing understanding of the physics and mechanics of their world.

Omar was initially an observer of the intense activity happening around the creek. He was deeply interested in what the four-year-old children were doing and he watched them closely. He did not engage with the materials, but simply observed. Later he moved to another spot along the creek and replicated what he had seen the older children doing. He used the different materials he had gathered, putting them in the water one at a time to see whether they would float. He watched them move down the stream and observed the way they performed in the water. He experimented in different places to test the current, and laid a leaf on the mud. Through this series of experiments Omar arrived at a variety of answers to his question about what floats and what does not.

How does engaging with natural processes such as gravity, water flow, melting, and freezing encourage children to experiment with a variety of approaches and solutions? How do you support children's engagement with natural processes?

INDICATOR 3: *The child applies strategies such as trial and error, comparing, sorting, classifying, and organizing to understand and find solutions.*

THREE OLD POTATOES

"I found a potato here."
"Is it a rock?"
"Let's check."

The children are weeding last year's potato bed, preparing it for tomorrow's planting of new potatoes. Terrell digs up something round and hard

in the soil and wonders what it is. The teacher suggests that they tap the side to see if it is a stone. When they find it is not hard enough to be a stone, she asks what they think it is. "A potato?!" they exclaim. They go on to find several more objects in the bed, which they proceed to test in the same way. Of those, two more are old potatoes from last year. Once

the bed has been dug and raked out, the children put away their tools and most head off for other activities. Terrell and Marcus remain behind. They take the three potatoes they've found and organize them on a landscape timber from smallest to largest. They poke them and notice that two are hard and one is very soft. Using their fingers, they squish the softest potato and say, "Ooh!" as it collapses on the wood.

STRATEGIES such as trial and error, comparing, sorting, classifying, and organizing are particularly suited to the kinds of investigations that happen outside. Often children come upon an interesting object or phenomenon and want to understand more about it. For example, are these round, brown things rocks, potatoes, or something else? They are an unexpected discovery, and there is no ready-made script to tell the children what they have found. The teacher makes an assumption relying on what she knows about rocks and potatoes and proposes that the children tap this thing with a trowel to see how hard it is. This kind of trial and error investigation is something children can understand and enjoy, and they get busy right away.

Once the potatoes have been identified through trial and error, the children recognize a second variable and sort the potatoes by size, lining them up in order from smallest to largest. Handling them in this way, the children realize how very soft the biggest one is compared to the others. This makes them want to squish it to see what will happen. Without any direct instruction beyond the teacher's initial suggestion to tap the object with the trowel, the children apply all of the strategies in the indicator on their own as they engage in meaningful reasoning and problem solving.

Children are interested in the qualities and attributes of the objects in their environment. Color, size, and shape are all qualities that children use to identify objects and distinguish among them. In this story, Terrell and Marcus explored the attributes of the objects they found in the potato bed to understand more about them. They were naturally using the skills of comparing, sorting, and classifying within the context of a real-life problem that mattered to them. They were intrinsically motivated and applied all the energy that comes with wanting to know. The teacher had not set this task for them; they had set it for themselves as part of an ongoing investigation and long-term project with which they and their classmates were involved for several months (see Potato Story, chapter 3). The kind of interest that builds within a community of children when they are involved with such long-term projects is very powerful. How much they want to know about potatoes (and many other things) will grow exponentially over the duration of the project, creating endless opportunities to refine their reasoning and problem-solving skills, both inside and outside.

BUTTERCUPS

Michele wonders to herself, "Are they all the same?"

Michele is sitting on the grass with three other girls. They are talking to each other and ignoring her. After a few minutes, she notices in the distance some small, yellow flowers and goes over to investigate. She leans down to look more closely at the first buttercups of the season. After studying them, she picks one, stands up, and holds it close to her face, checking to see how it smells. She then bends over and picks several more, examining them in her hand and counting and comparing the number of petals.

GRASSY AREAS and meadows offer children a myriad of detail and mystery when they have the opportunity to look at them closely. The round leaves of clover, the blossoms of spring wildflowers, the seed heads of grass, the invading dandelions—all call attention to themselves amid the blades of grass and beckon to children. A close-cropped lawn can become a treasure trove if it is simply not mowed for a while. Releasing a small or large field of grass to become a meadow will not only add the color and interest of flowers and seeds, but will attract the pollinating insects that feed on them. Butterflies will soon enrich the scene, and birds will come as well. All these gifts of nature invite investigation of the kind Michele is involved with: quiet, contemplative, restful, and intensely interesting. When a child can explore like this, she begins to ask questions: What is this? Is there another one like it? Which one is bigger? How many can I find?

Michele was feeling left out of the group. As her mind began to wander, her eyes scanned the grassy field and lighted on a bright yellow patch of flowers. Because she was outside, she could stand and leave the group to follow a new interest and thereby take initiative to make herself more comfortable. By moving to investigate the flowers, she took herself away from a social situation where she was not experiencing success. Instead, she pursued an intellectual investigation that interested her and one in which she could feel successful. Although in doing this, she was moving away from the other girls, her actions had the potential to help improve the other girls' connection by drawing their interest into her investigation. When this standard talks about solving problems, it is not referring to social problems per se. But social and intellectual development are closely linked and often overlap. By responding to a social challenge through intellectual curiosity Michele demonstrated real-life problem solving, engaging with this standard in a powerful way.

What is the role of diverse materials and time in children's development of problem-solving skills and strategies? What materials are available naturally in your outdoor space for children to use in a variety of ways? How much time do children have for their own explorations outdoors?

INDICATOR 4: *The child discusses, consults, and collaborates with other children and adults in working through questions and investigations.*

PRAYING MANTIS

"Preying mantises haf slisers fore arms."

It is springtime, and the children are noticing the many insects that come and go from the garden outside. Building on their initial interest, a month-long study evolves that includes observation, research in books, scientific drawings, movement and music activities, and eventually a play. Children select a particular insect to research based on their own interest. At the end of the month they display outside the drawings they have made to tell what they have learned. They also 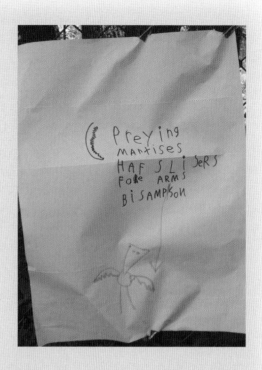 perform for the school community a play that they have written themselves, complete with costumes, sets, and small sips of fruit juice "nectar" for all the participating "insects."

CHILDREN ARE inevitably interested in insects and find them fascinating. There are so many of them and so many varieties. Some have wings and fly. Some have big back legs and hop. They may be electric blue or yellow or black. And each has a special and knowable way of making its way in the world by eating someone or something else. Insects also make wonderful sounds. Most insects are not harmful, but some are. This means that it is a good idea for children to know how to identify insects and to be able to enjoy those that are benign, such as butterflies and grasshoppers, and protect themselves from the ones that may not be, such as ticks and bees. The month-long investigation of insects illustrated here grew from the children's interest and was designed to respond to their particular questions and concerns. Gaining knowledge of insects in this fun and extensive way has many benefits, including contributing to children's ability to keep themselves safe.

Designing longer-term projects with children creates an efficient vehicle for discussion, consultation, and collaboration between children and between children and adults. The structure of this project required children to try many modes of exploration and expression around the study of insects. To find out as much as possible about the praying mantis, for example, Sampson not only looked at books and read stories, he also observed nature and did careful drawings. He also had a chance to apply the facts that he was learning through movement and music, "being" a praying mantis and experiencing from the inside what that might be like.

Such experiences lead children to develop empathy, a deeper understanding of the material, and crucially, more questions. The success of such studies depends on the educator correctly identifying the children's deep interest and must be constructed around the vivid themes that inspire them. Children want to understand their world—both the things they encounter that frighten them and those that delight them and give them joy. This story illustrates some of the many different ways you can support children in this area.

MULCH BUCKET

"Let's fill it up to the top!"

Shamika, Crystal, and Skyler notice some small pebbles and some sand in the mulch next to a low wooden wall. They squat down and examine the mulch more closely, talking together about what they find. They pick out some small pieces of rock. Holding these objects in their hands, they talk.

Shamika notices a large bucket next to them and throws her pebbles into it. Crystal and Skyler do the same. When they can find no more pebbles, they begin searching for twigs and leaves to add to the bucket. Finally, they pick up handfuls of mulch and add them to the bucket as well. Crystal then says, "Let's fill it up." They work together nonstop for fifteen minutes, drawing in a helper, and finally fill the very large bucket to the brim with mulch. Just then their teacher announces it is time to clean up. When they say, "But we . . . ," she interrupts their protest, saying, "Please dump it out and come inside." When the children resist again, "But . . . ," she offers, "You can do it again tomorrow."

THIS STORY is set in an outdoor environment with limited resources, but it is useful because it shows so clearly how children's play is supported when they can make use of loose parts of any kind. The ability for children to group and regroup themselves around ideas that interest them is enhanced outdoors where they can freely move about and come upon the raw materials of an endless variety of projects and investigations.

Shamika, Crystal, and Skyler were in a play yard that has few plants, trees, or other interesting materials to play with. Most of the surface area was covered with bark mulch. Yet, even in this relatively barren environment, the sharp eyes of the children discerned difference, and they began to investigate it. They picked out twigs, leaves, and small rocks from the surrounding mulch and examined them. Once they had a small collection of objects in their hands, Shamika noticed the bucket, the only prop in their area. Seeing it, she made the connection that it could hold their stuff.

Throwing their objects into the bucket led them to yet another idea, the challenge of filling the bucket. They discussed this option and agreed on a plan to do so. They had no tools, and it was hard work to fill this large bucket just with their hands. Nonetheless, they took their plan very seriously, carrying the increasingly heavy bucket to a place where the mulch was less compacted and easier to grab with their small hands. They persisted, and in the process used the words "more" and "less," "heavy" and "light," and "big" and "little," continually comparing and describing their work. By the end of their outdoor time, through collaboration and hard work, they filled the entire bucket, happily engaged with a learning activity they created for themselves with nothing more than a bucket.

Many teachers have been trained to think of outdoor time as unrelated to the curriculum and children's learning. Instead it is viewed as a break from the important work that happens inside. When teachers come to understand and value the depth and sophistication of the work children do in outdoor environments, they can do a better job recognizing and valuing the activities children engage in. They can also do a better job of provisioning outdoor environments with the things children need to engage in the important work and play that occurs there.

In this story, Shamika, Crystal, and Skyler were intensely discussing and problem solving together for the entire forty minutes of their outdoor time. They were focused on a task that they had set independently for themselves. They were negotiating together about how to meet their goal, naming, describing, sorting, and classifying the objects they were finding. They talked together, sharing, listening, and helping each other. While the task of filling a bucket seems initially unremarkable and not very interesting, it held many layers of learning. Shamika, Crystal, and Skyler had a limited range of tools and loose parts to choose from on their play yard and they used them creatively. They devised for themselves the task of filling a ten-gallon bucket.

This self-chosen activity allowed them to practice many important skills appropriate for their age group: naming, describing, sorting, classifying, estimating, goal setting, and evaluating. Their teacher would readily recognize these skills if she saw them displayed inside, but they were harder for her to see within the context of outdoor play. Seeing the reasoning, problem solving, and collaboration embedded in this activity requires careful observation by an educator and the right framework and set of expectations. Early learning standards provide this framework. The standards are a particularly valuable tool for interpreting and understanding what children do in the challenging, less familiar learning setting of the outdoors.

How does documenting children's work, questions, and discoveries help you develop a more supportive role in the outdoors?

Further Reflection

How might applying the reasoning and problem-solving standard affect your teaching outdoors?

In the natural world, children spontaneously explore the environment and identify problems. The outdoors comes primed for children to reason, problem solve, and figure things out. So many of the puzzles and mysteries that children discover outdoors and want to investigate have ready-made paths for them to follow in looking into what is really going on. When they see what they think might be a carrot in the garden, there is a real physical investigation they can pursue to find out. Their past experience planting a garden in this place motivates them to notice and follow the clue that presents itself through the fernlike leaves hiding under the invading ground ivy. The delicate leaves are a clear invitation to dig down into the soil and see whether, in fact, there is a carrot below.

In the same way, Madison has some understanding of the variables that may affect how the snow behaves and whether or not she will be able to make a snowball that will hold together. As she looks across her play yard, she sees the places where the variables can be tested: the ground, the wooden top of the outdoor blocks, places where the snow has collected and is in the shade, and places where it may be warming up in the sun. The environment thus supports her ability to reason. She can look around and see more than one approach to the problem she is trying to solve.

In an environment that is well aligned with children's need to figure things out, the role of the teacher is to observe what children are interested in, provide the materials and tools they need to support and extend their engagement, and offer thoughtful questions rather than answers.

For the things we have to learn before we can do, we learn by doing . . .
ARISTOTLE

Risk-Taking, Responsibility, and Confidence Standard

CHILDREN COME INTO THE WORLD hardwired to interact with the environment. Their sensory systems grow and develop by acting on and reacting to elements in the world around them. When stimulated by movement, infants gradually learn to track objects in space. When they hear sound, they are progressively able to locate the source. Infants are continually gathering information that allows them to understand and make sense of what is happening around them. They do this by moving, touching, looking, smelling, and listening. "Our first teachers . . . are our feet, our hands and our eyes," noted Jean-Jacques Rousseau (2003, 90).

Infants come into the world predisposed to this active mode of learning. Their approach to information gathering is concrete and experiential. They learn by engaging and responding to the environment in an ongoing process of exploring new and unfamiliar sights, sounds, and experiences. As children grow, their most effective means of learning about the world around them continues to be active, concrete, and experiential. Throughout their lives, whether it is reaching for a toy, taking a first step, or riding a bicycle, children's innate motivation to engage requires that they explore and venture into the unknown. All of their learning involves doing. They move themselves toward what they want or want to understand.

By acting, children continuously strive to answer the question, "What would happen if . . . ?" They cannot answer this question unless they try different approaches, demonstrate persistence, fail, and try again. It is only through experience that children build understanding and develop skills that enable them to become both competent and confident. This means that they must be able to act upon the world and then reflect on the impact of their actions. In addition, they must then have the opportunity to take those reflections and apply them to future experiences.

This ongoing process of acting, reflecting, then fine-tuning one's approach may appear to happen quickly and seamlessly, "in the blink of an eye." For example, a child who is unsteady standing on a log suddenly balances with confidence. A three-year-old who has demanded to be pushed on the swings since September, one morning, seemingly out of the blue, pumps herself. These milestones where children suddenly display new competence are exciting.

While such events seem to happen all by themselves, they actually represent a great deal of effort and courage on the part of the child. Such achievements require children to be willing to confront the unknown and, in many cases, to take considerable risks. They may fall off the log as they try to walk across it. Other children may tease them when they hesitate or become tentative at the top of the slide. They may trip and fall as they run, skinning a knee or scraping an elbow. By observing closely, teachers can see how challenging it is to gain new skills and better understand the process children go through to learn. Learning to ride a two-wheel bike or mixing just the right paints to make the perfect blue (see Making the Perfect Blue later in this chapter) require time, persistence, motivation, and the incorporation of new concepts and skills.

When situations are analyzed where the learning process is more visible and spans a longer period of time, the effort required becomes evident. The discrete steps and fine-tuning children engage in as they master complex skills are visible. A young child may take weeks or months to develop the balance, timing, and confidence to ride a two-wheel bike. The process often includes falling, stubbing a toe, or skinning a knee. Mastering the mechanics of riding a bike is a challenge that requires children to stretch, expand, and adjust what they are doing as they experience the results of their various actions. They develop the ability to make small and subtle adjustments to maintain their balance. Gradually, they learn to steer effectively and lean into the curves as they go around a corner. They gather speed, confidence, and the ability to navigate a variety of terrains.

Similarly, mixing paints to create a specific shade or color requires a great deal of trial and error and the learning of new skills—motor skills, intellectual skills, and aesthetic judgment. Children must experiment with and learn about basic color combinations. "What happens when I mix yellow with red? How can I make green?" From this foundation, they begin to explore more subtle variations and the distinct gradations they can achieve by adding just a little bit more of one color or another. This requires learning to control their pouring and their paintbrush to get just the desired amount of paint but not too much.

Although not often thought of in this way, this activity requires that children be willing to take some sizable risks. They may spill paint on themselves, the floor, or others. They may add too much paint and lose a beautiful color they have mixed and treasure. They may be unable to produce the exact color or shade that is their goal. So they risk being disappointed, frustrated, or maybe reprimanded if they end up making a mess. But by taking those risks, children also increase the likelihood that they will make new discoveries, experience deep satisfaction, and learn something new.

Young children's view of the world and how it works is continually stretched, expanded, and adjusted through opportunities to interact with their physical environment. By engaging in solving problems in real time, children get the information back that they need to understand the impact of their actions. This feedback allows children to continually discover new things about the world and about themselves. It is by attempting new things that children grow.

Learning is, at heart, a collaboration between children and their environment. To learn, they must engage and when children are young, much of that engagement is physical. Less than two generations ago, getting dirty, bumped, or bruised was considered natural, and a completely acceptable part of a normal, active childhood. In fact, children often touted cuts and scrapes as badges of honor, showing how brave they had been in the face of a particular challenge. Now, however, society increasingly tries to protect children from even superficial injuries.

The unrealistic belief that adults can and should protect children from all pain and harm is at odds with how children learn. A four-year-old proudly announces, "I fell twenty-nine times! It's the record!" He is owning his hard-won experience of learning to balance on a two-wheel bike. He understands intuitively, and so does his teacher, that falling is an inevitable part of developing physical competence. The confidence that he develops through taking acceptable risks allows him to learn motor planning and how to manage where his body is in space. The interaction between risk taking, confidence, and learning is fundamental for teachers to understand. It is at the heart of children's healthy growth and development.

Overview

Why is the risk-taking, responsibility, and confidence standard important for healthy child development?

Young children are active learners. They learn about the world and about themselves predominantly through their bodies, acting and interacting with others and with their environment. When asked to describe their goals, young children often state them in terms of their own physical competence: "I want to learn to pump so I can swing by myself." "I want to climb to the top of the structure." "I want to balance all the way around the stumps without falling." These examples of the real-world goals of some four-year-olds show how self-directed children are, and how they see themselves as competent and capable. They also show how motivated children are to become independent.

The risk-taking, responsibility, and confidence standard speaks directly to children's desire for autonomy and independence and education's role in supporting that goal. It addresses the process children engage in as they figure things out for themselves and work to refine their understanding of the world. This standard in particular involves approaches to learning that require special attention and support from you. To become independent, children must be allowed to confront, experience, and solve real-world problems. They must be supported in making mistakes and taking risks.

Children have to experience failing to recognize and understand success. They must experience falling as part of balancing and learning to run like the wind. By being allowed to experience frustration, they can contrast it with the elation they feel when they are deeply satisfied with their work. Although adults generally consider failure, falling, and frustration as negative and unpleasant and want to protect children from them, such experiences are valuable and necessary—and children really cannot be protected from them. They will confront these experiences throughout their lives and need to learn how to use, manage, and understand them within the context of their own learning.

Teachers have an important role here. It is the teacher's job to structure the environment in such a way that children can make independent choices, pursue different ideas, articulate their own questions, try new things, and make mistakes. Letting children follow their own interests, use materials in different ways, set their own goals, and make mistakes can be challenging. Solving real problems can be a messy and unpredictable process. But, taking risks to find out what works and what doesn't fine-tunes the ability to think creatively and increases confidence. To paraphrase John Dewey, we only think when we are confronted with a problem.

Children are particularly motivated to solve problems they have set for themselves. They are also more likely to stretch themselves and take productive risks with their learning in situations where they are exploring their own problems and answering their own questions. This speaks to a unique and inspiring role for the teacher as one who is supporting and enhancing learning rather than prescribing and directing it.

Pragmatic View

How do states and national early childhood organizations classify risk taking, responsibility, and confidence?

Risk taking, responsibility, and confidence are less frequently mentioned and perhaps less well understood by teachers than many of the other standards treated in this book. Risk taking in particular is mentioned infrequently. When it is mentioned, risk taking is sometimes paired with flexibility and sometimes paired with problem solving. Confidence and responsibility, which are the natural outcomes of the experience of taking appropriate risks, are also mentioned infrequently. But, in our experience and observation of young children learning, we see these three standards as vital to healthy child development. We also see these three standards as inextricably linked to one another. When children can take appropriate risks commensurate with their level of independence, an important process is set in motion. They begin to formulate their own questions and organize their activities around exploring and answering those questions. They apply strategies like trial and error and the manipulation of objects to gain specific knowledge. In this way, they take responsibility for their own learning and develop confidence in their own abilities.

The outdoors is particularly well suited to offer children the time and space they need to pursue these investigations. Because it is a self-regulating system, it is an ongoing demonstration of cause and effect. As such, it allows children to experience the relationship between action and reaction, essential for developing judgment. Because it is ever changing and engages children's curiosity, the natural world inspires children to ask new questions daily as they notice and observe changes and see new things. They see the sky darken as the clouds cover the sun. They see a low-hanging branch and wonder what it would feel like to sit on it and bounce up and down. They notice leaves turning color and falling to the ground and try to catch them in midair. They notice a garter snake sunning on a rock. These phenomena invite children to take a closer look, ask questions, and wonder what is going on.

Applied View

What are the observable behaviors or indicators that demonstrate children engaging with the risk-taking, responsibility, and confidence standard?

As discussed in chapter 2, curiosity is the primary engine that drives learning. Curious children develop their own questions and strive to answer them, using the environment as a resource. To do this, they have to play and work in environments that let them explore and experiment. They have to be allowed to take appropriate risks. The challenge for the teacher is to promote this curiosity and risk taking while also keeping children safe. Understanding the risk-taking, responsibility, and confidence standard allows teachers to systematically plan appropriate activities and environments. Having clear indicators that show what these approaches to learning look like in action facilitates this planning. Clear indicators also provide helpful language for discussing standards with other teachers, parents, and children. The indicators help clarify the desired outcomes so teachers can both discuss them and design and plan the environment in a way that supports those outcomes for children.

We have synthesized from the observable behaviors articulated in the various state standards four representative indicators of risk taking, responsibility, and confidence for three- to five-year-olds:

1. The child chooses appropriate physical, social, and cognitive challenges, demonstrating growing awareness of his or her own ability.

2. The child sets goals and follows through on plans with increasing independence.

3. The child communicates his or her own ideas and opinions in interactions with others—both peers and adults.

4. The child expresses delight and satisfaction when solving problems or completing tasks.

Experiencing the Risk-Taking, Responsibility, and Confidence Standard in the Outdoors

INDICATOR 1: *The child chooses appropriate physical, social, and cognitive challenges, demonstrating growing awareness of his or her own ability.*

WINTER WOODS

"It's hard to get up, but I am not scared."

The children and their teacher are on a winter walk, following a trail through the woods. Felix spots a tree trunk lying in the snow with a sturdy limb extending up into the air. He reaches out and takes hold of the limb, using it to balance himself as he steps up onto the snow-covered trunk. He plays with the slippery surface, letting his feet slide across the ice, jumping into the snow when he can no longer maintain his balance. He immediately hops back up and tries again, repeating this effort and staying upright longer each time he tries.

AS OFTEN HAPPENS OUTSIDE, Felix has found a challenge tailor-made to his interests and abilities. When children have access to natural areas, their physical explorations often lead them to natural climbing and play structures fitted exactly to their own bodies. They may find a ravine that lets them practice walking downhill or a little creek that lets them practice jumping across. They often walk along the streamside to find the distance that is just right for them. They get to practice balance, coordination, judgment, and motor planning, all within an exciting and meaningful context. Though approved for three- to five-year-olds, the rungs of a manufactured play structure are "one size fits all," and provide a consistent, predictable experience. Woods, fields, and other natural places offer experiences at many different levels of challenge, allowing individual children to find just the right challenge for their own needs and abilities. What children engage with can be different each day as they grow and develop their skills. Their focus is sharpened by the novelty.

Felix identified a task or interest he wanted to pursue. He investigated it on his own to learn more about what it involved. Children who are allowed the freedom to explore generally have a good understanding of their own abilities. They choose a setting for practicing their skills that offers both the challenge and the support they need. For Felix, this meant choosing a task that was fun for him, challenged his growing ability to balance, and provided him with the safety net of a handhold and a soft place to land in the snow if he fell. Each time he stood on the log, he got better at balancing; he acquired new information about timing and about positioning his body, increasing his confidence, judgment, and skills. Felix demonstrated both judgment and control by designing his balancing activity in a staged way that offered him a chance to practice holding on and letting go, standing alternately on flatter and steeper parts of the log. Felix understood very quickly that the log was slippery and he became equally interested in both balancing and falling. He played with the notion of falling by sliding his feet on the slippery surface and jumping off when he began to lose his balance. He experimented with the variables that might cause him to fall. His experience provides a good example of how children understand and engage with the risks of activities like balancing and learn from them.

TIRE ROLL

"I'm going to push the tire down with Wesley. I go up here where it really rolls. I put sand in it and it's going around in circles."

A parent has provided a tire for the day for use on the play yard. Morgan has been rolling it on the level concrete path along the fence. She has to push it hard so that it will roll fast enough on the flat ground to stay upright. Wesley watches her with interest and suggests that they go up on the hill and roll it together. They roll it up the hill, away from the other children, and practice sending it back and forth between them. Gradually, they increase the distance, making suggestions to each other about ways to make it roll faster and straighter. After doing this for a while, Morgan goes and gets a cupful of sand and pours it into the bottom of the tire. "Here it comes!" she calls to Wesley as she sends it rolling his way.

SOME TASKS are easier and more fun to do with another person. Rolling a tire or throwing a ball is an example of an experience that engages children with each other. Working with another person often provides children with encouragement, feedback, and modeling that enables them to stretch themselves in new ways. It also creates social challenges and opportunities for language development through negotiating, turn taking, making plans, and questioning each other's ideas.

Collaboration involves an exchange of ideas and sharing of skills that leads to new and valuable learning in all areas. Because they can follow their own interests and create their own games, collaborating provides children with opportunities to work in different ways with each other. When materials are open ended, children have to talk and work to share their ideas and develop a script for playing together. They can be observed creating very sophisticated scenarios from very simple and ambiguous materials. In the outdoors, children can readily create activities of their own design using the loose parts that are available—twigs, stumps, leaves, buckets, or, as in this story of Morgan and Wesley, a tire.

Morgan experimented with the tire, rolling it first on the path by herself and running to retrieve it when it rolled away. Each time she experimented with different strategies. She rolled it faster and slower, holding it differently before pushing it. As she practiced, her technique improved. She was able to get it to stay upright for longer rolls.

Wesley watched her with interest as she worked. He suggested that they roll it together on the hill where they would have a slope to work with. Together, they pushed the tire up the hill, talking and planning, choosing a spot with a nice grade and away from other children and their activities. They began by standing close together, rolling it back and forth and encouraging one another, cheering when it rolled the whole way between them and laughing when it didn't. As they mastered one distance, they increased the challenge by moving in small steps farther and farther apart.

Their game continued for some time, with lots of conversation, exchange of ideas, and collaboration. Morgan then added a new element, scooping sand into the bottom of the tire before rolling it to Wesley. They both checked the sand after each roll to see how much stayed in the tire and how much fell out. With nothing but a tire and one another, Morgan and Wesley created a fun game that involved skill and practice, aiming and rolling the tire upright and maintaining control of it. They got better and better at it, extending the distance and increasing the challenge, learning the best way to do it successfully as they worked together.

In our risk-averse society, how are you an advocate for the benefits of compelling and appropriate physical challenges for children on outdoor play yards?

INDICATOR 2: *The child sets goals and follows through on plans with increasing independence.*

MAKING THE PERFECT BLUE

"Now I need to make the perfect blue for me!"

It's a beautiful fall day. The leaves are glowing with many shades of yellow, orange, and green. The easel is set up outside for the children to paint. Rebecca begins painting on one side of the easel from paints that have been pre-mixed for the children to use. She says aloud, "I don't have the perfect green." Amelia, who Is about to start painting on the opposite side of the easel,

offers to mix "the perfect green" for the younger child. She finds an empty paint jar and selects the large gallon-size of yellow paint, and then the green paint, and pours some of each into the jar. She mixes it carefully. Rebecca watches her intently. When the brilliant green is mixed, Amelia asks her if that's the color she wants. Rebecca nods. Amelia offers, "Do you want it lighter?" and when Rebecca agrees, Amelia adds small amounts of white paint. She mixes the paint after every addition until they agree they have the perfect shade of green. Amelia places the paint jar in the tray at Rebecca's spot then, turning back to the paint, exclaims, "Now I need to make the perfect blue for me!"

AS NOTED EARLIER, outdoor environments are more forgiving of mess and mistakes than most indoor settings. In this story the teacher recognized and built on this attribute of the outdoors. Knowing that children love to paint, and love to mix paint, she gave the children time earlier in the year to practice pouring from large containers, mixing paint, and cleaning up after using the paints. By practicing these requisite skills, she equipped the children to become increasingly independent throughout the year.

The story takes place in October, and the easel has been set up with multiple sheets of paper so the children can paint on their own, remove their work when they decide they are finished, and hang it up to dry. In the easel tray, the teacher placed a variety of colors and a container of water. On the ground next to the easel, she placed a container with many sizes of brushes, another container with more water, and gallon jugs of every color of paint, in case children want to mix a different color or shade. The outdoor easel has been set up to allow children maximum freedom and maximum responsibility; the two go hand in hand.

The opportunity to take control of a project, from the initial idea to the final cleanup, is an important experience for children. It allows them to experience the whole process, gain confidence, develop independence, and practice their skills. Outdoors, the children can paint without the worry that they will upset the adult if they spill a little paint or water. This encourages both the teacher and the child to relax and focus on the process.

Amelia stopped to look at Rebecca's painting before starting her own. Rebecca's assessment that she did not have the perfect green sparked Amelia's interest in the problem. The setting enabled Amelia to be independent and feel capable. This gave her confidence to take on the role of helper, a role she committed to very seriously. Amelia spent a good five minutes talking with Rebecca and experimenting with the paint until she produced a shade that met with Rebecca's approval. Meeting this goal required a lot of pouring, mixing, and conversation as the two girls consulted. All of this effort to reach the goal seemed to inspire Amelia to continue mixing and pouring. She then set a new goal. With confidence and independence, she proceeded to mix "just the right shade of blue" for herself.

THE BRIDGE

"A bridge!"

The preschool children have been studying transportation. Every vehicle in the school's collection is on display. Inside, there is a dump truck next to the collection of books in the reading corner. A box of vehicles of all sorts is next to a carpet laid out with roads and stop signs. Vehicles to scale are available in the area where children are playing with the big blocks as well as smaller vehicles where the smaller unit blocks are used. Stencils depicting vehicles in profile are set out at a table with markers and pencils for tracing around the edges

of the shapes. Small plastic cars and trucks are at the paint table where children can dip their wheels in different colors and create trails and designs across large sheets of paper. A variety of books are available to the children depicting vehicles, space travel, and construction machines.

The opportunity to explore various means of transportation is also available outside. Children can ride on a variety of plastic vehicles. Buckets with sponges are set out for children to stage a car wash. Large traffic signs encourage children to create streets and explore the rules of the road. On a raised wooden platform, children have access to big blocks where they can pursue ideas similar to the work they are doing in their indoor classroom. The environment—indoors and out—is saturated with rich opportunities to explore and understand transportation.

One day, while working in the big blocks area, Chad sets a board atop two slightly separated blocks, and with great excitement, recognizes it as a bridge. From this discovery, a deep interest in bridges and bridge building evolves in the group of children. They begin sharing what they know about bridges and what they want to know. They begin drawing bridges, reading about bridges, and acting out bridge stories such as The Three Billy Goats Gruff. Several children suggest the goal of "building our own bridge." Other children say this is silly or just not possible. After several exploratory discussions with teachers, it becomes clear to the children that they do indeed have the skills and strategies they need to build a real bridge on their own play yard. They happily shout "A bridge!" upon completion.

CHILDREN HAVE BIG IDEAS and passions related to content that can take time to surface and explore. Long-term projects like building a bridge can enliven outdoor spaces, where such projects can be worked on for a period of weeks or months without interfering with other needs of the group. A great deal of research, planning, drawing, measuring, cutting, sanding, and nailing was involved in building the bridge. The children were able to tackle each challenge with confidence under the umbrella of their enthusiasm and understanding of the project. Taken in stages, each part of the project offered children opportunities to problem solve and apply their skills to a very concrete goal. Following an idea over a long period of time and participating in such a complex project builds confidence and allows children to practice new skills.

The bridge was a two-month study that, on first glance, might have seemed too ambitious to many teachers. But long-term projects evolving from children's own interests provide a powerful vehicle for meeting early learning standards. They provide a structure that actually makes teaching and learning more fluid and more meaningful. Feeling comfortable taking on long-term projects requires examining and understanding the separate pieces involved. Viewing the pieces as chapters, or mini units, makes it easier to see how doable they are.

Over the two months of working on this bridge, the children developed an understanding of the principles and ideas involved. They practiced woodworking, built models with blocks, and measured off and flagged a space outside. They visited bridges in the community and talked to engineers. From this fieldwork structured by their teacher, and from the innumerable conversations and discussions they had about it, they were able to take increasing initiative and responsibility for the design, building, and enjoyment of their very own bridge.

What was the same and what was different about the role the two teachers played in the stories Making the Perfect Blue *and* The Bridge? *How did each teacher express confidence in the children's abilities to move forward with their ideas? How do you express confidence in children's abilities?*

INDICATOR 3: *The child communicates his or her own ideas and opinions in interactions with others—both peers and adults.*

THE LADYBUG

"Don't worry. I will take you to the garden."

Tristan notices a ladybug that has landed on his sleeve and is crawling up his arm. He watches it for a few moments, but then would like to get it off. He calls to the children nearby for help. Alex and Jessica are both delighted by the ladybug and reassure Tristan that it will not hurt him, and that they will get it off. After several attempts to get the ladybug to crawl onto one of their fingers, Jessica is able to transfer the insect from Tristan's sleeve to her finger to her cupped hands. Speaking softly to the ladybug, she says, "Don't worry. I will take you to the garden." She walks carefully toward the vegetable bed, cradling the ladybug in her hands.

UNPLANNED INTERACTIONS between children and animals, including insects, occur frequently outside. These encounters are exciting and provide unique learning opportunities. Children need protocols that tell them what to do when they find insects, arachnids, amphibians, and other living things. Having information about how to stay safe and what to expect outside gives children confidence and helps them feel secure.

Children look to their teachers as guides for how to react and what to do. Teachers transmit their values to the children in their care: some model fear or discomfort (for example, by recoiling or killing insects), while others model curiosity, engagement, confidence, respect, and responsibility. The latter group will find these attitudes expressed by the children they work with. It is therefore very important that you take an active interest in learning about and developing comfort with the living creatures they may find outside. By understanding them, and knowing which can be safely investigated and which should be left alone, you can be prepared to engage safely with the outdoors.

This story depicts two children, Alex and Jessica, who felt comfortable and confident with the ladybug, and another child, Tristan, who felt more tentative. As he grew increasingly uncomfortable, Tristan effectively communicated his misgivings and concerns about having the ladybug on his sleeve. He was able to express his feelings and ask his friends for help. They responded positively and both reassured and helped him with his request. The teacher had created a climate of trust by modeling empathy, active listening, and problem solving. As a result, in this situation, the children were better able to communicate their ideas and concerns openly without fear of being criticized or teased. The communication and interpersonal skills these children learned from their teacher allowed them to function with greater independence and help one another instead of relying solely on their teacher to solve their problems.

THE TREE PLANTING

"There!"

It's Playground Work Day. Marco and his dad arrive just in time to help plant one of the playground's new young trees. With two other adults, they dig the hole and check the planting depth by placing the root-ball into the hole at various intervals. Each time, Marco bends down to see if the top of the root-ball is level with the ground or if it's still too high. When the hole is finally deep enough, his father helps Marco situate the tree into its new home.

He and his dad step back and evaluate whether the tree's trunk is straight. They then fill the hole, stomp the soil firmly into place, noting that it requires more soil around its base and adding it. Feeling satisfied, the adults move on to the next tree. Marco, however, remains behind and studies the tree for a few moments. He then moves to the dirt pile and returns with a shovelful of soil that he deposits at the base of the tree. He does this several times before standing back, evaluating his work, and declaring the job complete. "There!" he exclaims with pride.

ACTIVITIES that allow young children to participate in doing real work and contribute their own judgment to the outcome support the development of mathematical thinking skills. Such activities are readily available outside where children can not only dig and plant, but build with natural materials and gather, sort, count, and compare natural objects. Experience with nonstandard measurement creates a context for more refined applications of both nonstandard and standard measurement.

One of the basic judgments children are making in their work and play is that of "enough" and "not enough." Marco decided there was not enough soil, so he took the initiative to correct the situation and make it enough. Eventually numbers will be attached to judgments such as these. Wide experience with handling and thinking about concrete materials gives children a solid foundation in mathematical thinking and the confidence to make the kind of judgment this youngster is engaged with.

Marco, who was only three, came to his school's workday eager to participate and contribute. He wanted to help with the work modeled by parents, teachers, and volunteers all around him. By participating firsthand in the whole process of planting the tree, Marco experienced each step involved and understood its place in the process. With his new big-picture understanding, he demonstrated a sense of ownership around making sure that the result met his expectation of how it should look and be. Having decided that the tree needed more soil, he was able to take the initiative to remedy the situation because the environment had been provisioned and structured so that he could take that responsibility.

In planning for the workday, the volunteers had made sure to have tools in a variety of sizes suitable for all of the participants, including the youngest ones. In addition, they had generous and accessible supplies of planting soil and mulch. By having all these tools and materials accessible for children as well as adults, Marco's coworkers were telling him that his contribution mattered, and that they wanted him to be involved. This allowed him to develop his own ideas, opinions, and judgments about what was going on, and to take the initiative to act. This story shows how capable and competent even a three-year-old can be given the right circumstances and a structure that allows him time to develop an idea and make decisions about it.

In the first story, what do you imagine made it possible for Tristan, Jessica, and Alex to develop and demonstrate such confidence in communicating and moving forward with their own ideas? What about Marco in the second story? When have the children you teach shown similar confidence?

INDICATOR 4: *The child expresses delight and satisfaction when solving problems or completing tasks.*

THE BIG PUSH

"I did it!"

Eliza and two other children are riding trikes in the school yard, using the gentle slope at the back of the yard to create a faster ride. The children each take turns riding down the hill, cheering for one another. They then push their trikes back to the top of the hill. Eliza, who is the smallest, has

chosen a large two-seater tricycle that is heavy and difficult to push. She places her hands at either side of the back rim and digs her heels in, pushing it ahead of her. Soon, the front wheel turns out to the right. She stops, analyzes the problem, then straightens the front wheel. When she begins to push again, the wheel turns to the left, again taking her off course. Again she straightens it, and continues pushing. Finally she reaches the top of the hill and with a big smile, exclaims, "I did it!" She then takes off down the slope for another ride.

THE OUTDOORS provides lots of physical challenges for children that are crucial for healthy development. Children sometimes select physical tasks that may look too ambitious for them. But, if given enough time, teachers are likely to see that the tasks children choose are within their comfort and ability zone and provide the right level of challenge. Children can only become competent if adults let them practice and stretch their current abilities. It is by stretching and testing themselves that they develop judgment, decision making, and the ability to manage appropriate risk.

Increasingly, teachers face the unrealistic cultural expectation that children should be completely safe at all times. This is an impossible and unhelpful expectation. A continuum of risk, challenge, and safety is inherent in living. Teachers need to assess and support children taking appropriate risks so that the children gain the experience they need to develop competence. Children need practice, repetition, and the opportunity to make mistakes. Play yards that allow for a diversity of experience and abilities can more often offer just the right level of risk and challenge at just the right time for each child.

Experiences like Eliza's are challenging both for the child and for the teacher who is supervising her. Since healthy development requires that children challenge themselves and take risks, teachers must support them in doing this important work. Before deciding whether to intervene, teachers must use professional judgment to assess the situation. Sometimes this involves trusting children and their judgment a little more and watching them a little longer than is comfortable. By using good judgment, you can support children in taking the risks they need to take to advance their development.

Eliza took on a big challenge for herself. She selected the largest, heaviest trike, and her goal was to push it all the way up the slope all by herself. This required both persistence and continuous problem solving as she determined how to control the front wheel to get the tricycle to roll straight ahead. She persevered on her own, and although it was very difficult, she did not appear discouraged and did not want anyone's help.

Teachers often focus exclusively on the difficulties of the challenge itself, rather than on the whole of the child's experience. How children manage a challenge, and the decisions they make once they have selected a challenge, are critical parts of the process they are involved with. Given the time, children may find creative and unexpected ways to manage the task or they may change and redefine the task to something more manageable for themselves. Each instance of resetting the front tire required Eliza to observe, assess, make judgments, and develop a plan. In the end she was able to accomplish exactly what she set out to do.

What is the moral in this story? It is that the bigger the challenge, the bigger the satisfaction a child experiences when completing it.

RUNNING RACE

"Did you see how fast I run?"

The children line up together and wait for their teacher to holler, "Ready, Go!" At her shout, they burst from the line and run a hundred yards to the stone wall at the end. They respond to the big open space by swinging their arms, their giant strides taking them faster and faster to the end. Krista's smile lights up her face and she exclaims, "Did you see how fast I run?" Krista is flying! She runs the length of the field a number of times, each time pushing herself to run as fast and as hard as she can.

CHILDREN LOVE TO MOVE. Given the opportunity, they enjoy exerting a lot of energy in activities like running. At a time in which teachers are deeply aware of children's need for physical exercise, it is important to seek out as many opportunities as possible for children to discover the joys of being active. This group of children is lucky to have a teacher who almost daily makes use of the big green field next to the play yard. She takes the group of children across the grass and structures a number of different old-fashioned challenges: hop on one foot, run backward, turn in circles, and run in pairs holding hands with another child. All these simple directives challenge children to try new things, stretch their abilities, and increase their stamina and strength while having fun together.

Both of these stories illustrate situations where children are doing something challenging. Many teachers would worry that Eliza might hurt herself pushing such a large trike or that Krista or another child might trip and fall, racing so fast. What do you perceive as the possible risks and benefits of allowing children to pursue challenging activities like these?

This story shows the pure exhilaration children experience when they are given opportunities and the space to move without restriction. Krista smiled and laughed with her friends throughout the whole experience, delighting in the feel of her body and her sense of her own ability.

A running race is an experience that used to be much more common for children. However, these days, there is not often space to run like this either at home or in early childhood settings. To compensate for this loss of open space, look for places in your community that offer children wide-open spaces and the chance to develop their bodies in this free and fun way. Children in larger spaces are likely to demonstrate the kind of satisfaction the children in Krista's class exhibited as they problem solved their way through the puzzles posed by their teacher of running backward, hopping on one foot, and adjusting their speed to be able to run together in pairs. Such physical challenges are endlessly fascinating and satisfying for children, whether the challenges are set by teachers, as here, or by the children themselves.

Further Reflection

How might applying the risk-taking, responsibility, and confidence standard affect your teaching outdoors?

Children are doers and discoverers. They are at their best when they can act upon their world directly and see what happens as a result. When the environment holds possibilities, uncertainties, and ambiguities for them to explore, it encourages their experimentation. The outdoors provides the perfect place for this mode of learning. It invites children to be active by offering them endless things to explore and figure out.

As they interact with the world around them, which is so new to them, and seek to discover and understand its secrets, children are continually venturing into the unknown. This is how they learn, and although adults do not usually think of it this way, this learning requires a certain amount of courage to take the risks involved in exploring and trying new things. Throughout their lives, children will continually confront new problems and situations that stretch them to act and apply their skills in novel ways. To be willing to take the risks these situations present, they rely on their growing confidence and judgment. Children's confidence and judgment are developed by taking appropriate risks all along the way as they grow.

Sustaining young children's natural dispositions toward wonder, problem solving, and investigation is important and exciting work. These dispositions fuel children's learning throughout their schooling and throughout their lives. To be able to experiment productively, try new things, and make discoveries, children need opportunities to make choices and pursue their own interests. In other words, children thrive when they can be responsible for their own learning. When you provide an environment that encourages choice, inquiry, investigation, and independence, you help strengthen these essential attitudes toward learning and reinforce children's confidence.

In balancing on the snowy log, Felix extended himself beyond his known experience to try something new and exciting. In doing so, he took the risk of falling. Marco added soil after the adults decided the tree-planting job was complete, taking on a new level of responsibility for the tree. In doing so, he risked being told by the adults to stop what he was doing or that he was wrong. In trying to safely move the ladybug off Tristan's sleeve, Jessica took the initiative to help Tristan and protect the ladybug. She risked accidentally hurting the insect or further upsetting Tristan, but she proceeded with confidence.

Learning requires that children take action. Whether they succeed or fail at what they are trying to do, each experience is useful, as it expands their storehouse of knowledge. Over time and through a diversity of experience, children continuously refine their judgment and increase their confidence. In this way, they build a resilient attitude essential for lifelong learning that will help them whether they are three or ninety-three years old.

That is what learning is. You suddenly understand something
you've understood all your life, but in a new way.
DORIS LESSING

Reflection, Interpretation, and Application Standard

THE OUTDOORS IS OVERFLOWING with raw material for thought. There are flowers to smell, leaves to touch, birds to watch, sand to feel. For young children, whose learning needs are so concrete, the outdoors offers an endless resource of changing events and diverse materials. So much of what children see and experience outdoors is fresh and new to them. It engages their bodies and senses as tools for discovery, investigation, and understanding. It supports their unique learning style and their need for direct physical experience. This intense engagement invites children to reflect on what they are seeing, to work to interpret and make sense of it, and then to extend their thinking by applying what they learn to their next discovery.

To support children's active hands-on learning style, teachers must recognize and value process. Rather than emphasizing finished products, your role is to provide rich experiences for children that offer opportunities to make discoveries, observe changes, and feel unhurried as they reflect on what they are doing and seeing. For example, in creating a preschool garden with children, adults can become overly focused on the product, a bed of seedlings in orderly rows. Harnessing children to make this happen can be frustrating because much of the rich learning children do in the garden evolves in a more organic way. Children may discover a roly-poly bug or a potato from last year in the soil and linger to look for more. They may find a worm or a pretty stone they want to study. They may be captivated by the feel of the soil or the new experience of using a shovel, and want to practice digging. They may follow a butterfly as it moves from plant to plant through the garden. Pulling them back from such vibrant, compelling, in-the-moment learning experiences takes a lot of your energy. It also interrupts the real learning that is taking place. Instead, if you anticipate and include room for these unscripted and important encounters, you create just the right environment for reflection, interpretation, and application.

Overview

Why is the reflection, interpretation, and application standard important for healthy child development?

Young children are continuously struggling to make sense of their experiences. To do this, they construct theories to explain their impressions and perceptions. They then apply these theories to new experiences to see if they work. This process of taking experience, reflecting on it, interpreting its meaning, and applying it to new contexts is the child's essential work. This is how children continually add to and refine the conceptual framework they are building.

Young children process information differently from adults. They most often order and structure their understanding of what they see and experience through play. Play is a vital component of children's learning. It is through play that children actively process their experiences, test out their understandings, refine their theories, and apply new ideas.

Pragmatic View

How do states and national early childhood organizations classify reflection, interpretation, and application?

While reflection, interpretation, and application do not generally appear together in state standards, we have grouped them here because they are best understood as interconnected steps. In our experience, children engage with these three approaches to learning in a unified way as they process information and learn from their experiences.

Understanding each of these terms individually helps the understanding of how they work together. Reflection involves recapturing experience to think about it again or from a new perspective and with new depth. Children often reflect on their experiences as they play, engaging in dialogue, thinking (silently or aloud), asking questions, or conversing with others. Interpretation involves children in expressing what they have learned and exploring it further. They pretend, engage in role play, and represent their growing understanding through models, structures, stories, illustrations, music, and movement. These multiple expressive languages help children process and interpret experience. Application allows children to take these new interpretations and use what they have learned in a new context, generally at a more complex level than before. Reflection, interpretation, and application are deeply interrelated and need to be viewed in this light. They are the means by which children construct a conceptual framework for approaching experience, one that over time becomes increasingly sophisticated, refined, detailed, and precise.

Applied View

What are the observable behaviors or indicators that demonstrate children engaging with the reflection, interpretation, and application standard?

In reviewing indicators and observable behaviors that relate to the reflection, interpretation, and application standard, two vital elements are exposed. The first is the essential role of play in children's learning and processing. The second is time. Children need to feel unhurried as they think and sort things out. It takes time to pursue the process involved in remembering past events, thinking about what they mean, and sifting through the content of one's experience to apply parts of it to what comes next. Such a process is all of a piece and needs adequate time and space to unfold. The observable behaviors emphasize wondering and exploring, and explicitly do not mention getting the right answer or producing the right product as the goal or indicator that the standard is being met. This is because this standard is uniformly about the importance of process and the child's ability to engage in it as an approach to learning.

We have synthesized from the observable behaviors articulated in the various state standards three representative indicators of reflection, interpretation, and application for three- to five-year-olds:

1. The child relates past experience to new situations, generating ideas, increasing understanding, and making predictions.

2. The child speculates and demonstrates a beginning understanding of motivations and intentions, and what others are thinking.

3. The child uses play, representation, and discussion to process information and apply ideas.

Experiencing the Reflection, Interpretation, and Application Standard in the Outdoors

INDICATOR 1: *The child relates past experience to new situations, generating ideas, increasing understanding, and making predictions.*

THE LICHEN

"Look at these teeny, tiny flowers!"

Terrel has been digging in the raised garden beds at his school. As he and the other children finish up their work, they hang their tools where they go on the fence. Terrel turns to leave the garden, but stops short when he spots something brilliant red on one of the cedar boards edging the garden beds. He calls out to Rowan: "Hey, look at this!" Together, they bend down and look more closely, wondering aloud whether the red dots are tiny bugs or flowers. Their teacher joins them, saying, "Look what you found!" She listens to their conversation, takes note of what they have observed, and then asks, "What else do you notice?"

THE MINIATURE WORLD that Terrel found on the cedar log is ephemeral. Like many natural phenomena, it may change or disappear quickly. Was it there yesterday? Will it still be there tomorrow? This is the kind of mystery that captures children's imagination and prompts questions, dialogue, predictions, and investigations.

The props and prompts of the natural world are always evolving, shifting, and changing. This means that the outdoors is particularly expansive in the scope of opportunities it provides children for reflection, interpretation, and application. Teachers need to make sure that children have unscheduled time and space to wander about and stumble on such interesting and beautiful events as Terrel did.

These events are something you cannot manufacture and preplan for children as a lesson for the day. Rather, they appear as teachable moments that fuel children's desire to understand what is going on. Children's interests provide entry points for deeper conversations. Your role in these conversations is to help children articulate their questions, refine their observations, and relate their current activity to their prior experience and learning.

Exploring and talking with children in this way is particularly rich. It concentrates on the process the children are engaged in rather than on a perceived need to provide information or supply the answers to their questions. This kind of conversation is possible only when teachers ensure that the outdoor environment includes unscripted events that can unfold on their own.

Terrel and the other children had been working in the garden for a couple of weeks—yet it is only on this particular day that the miniature world that has been growing on the cedar log catches his eye. The flowers had reached a certain vivid red that pulled him in. Terrel doesn't know what they are, where they came from, or what they are doing. Will they still be as red tomorrow or will they open, fade, and then the show will be over? His need to explore and answer this question will motivate him to check back to see what happens. He will want to follow the story that the fungus presents. His teacher cultivated his interest by listening to his questions and ideas, reflecting with him on what he sees, and letting him continue to wonder and gather information to answer his own questions in his own time. In this way she encouraged him to look more closely, apply his experience to make predictions about what may happen next, and follow up with more observation to check his predictions against what he can see firsthand. She was not worried about whether he was right or wrong in his answers. She was much more concerned with his thinking process and his ability to generate ideas.

PUSSY WILLOW

"Is it like this one?"

It is outdoor time and Sage is heading out to play. Her path takes her under the branches of a pussy willow tree. She notices that some of the furry gray catkins have opened, showing their bright yellow anthers. She stops to take a closer look. As she investigates, her teacher joins her and asks her to describe what she is seeing. Sage notices aloud that not all of the buds are open. Some are tightly closed, others partially open, and some are fully burst and bright. Her teacher listens to her observations and then asks her if they are all different or if there are any that look just the same. "Is it like this one?"

THE SEQUENCE of bud to flower to seed offers myriad learning opportunities for children and teachers, starting in the early spring. The pussy willow is a plant that often fascinates children, who love to stroke its soft, fuzzy catkins. Sage returned to the pussy willow every day, noticing that the fuzzy gray catkins gradually opened into colorful bursts like fireworks. Her teacher helped extend Sage's experience by looking carefully with her, comparing the different stages, asking which one she thinks came first, second, and third, and wondering what will happen next. The learning potential of natural phenomenon for helping children understand a sequence of events is that they can actually watch the sequence unfold over time.

Sage was playing on a yard that was carefully designed and planned to offer children firsthand experiences of seasonal change and natural process. The concrete path meandered through trees and shrubs that bloom at different times of year. Flowers of all shapes, sizes, and colors and foliage with a range of color, texture, and form are available for the children to observe and touch. The trees and shrubs bear interesting fruits and seeds that the children can watch develop. The plants were selected carefully with young children in mind.

Such diversity and richness inspires children to engage with all their senses, notice changes, and wonder what will happen next. Teachers can help children as they are making meaning of what they see and sense by listening closely and encouraging the children to explore their ideas. Given the opportunity, children want variously to talk about what they are seeing, draw it, paint it, make models of it, and include elements from the environment in their imaginary play. All of these activities support deeper engagement with the kinds of questions and ideas that prompted Sage to stop and look more closely at the pussy willow plant.

How does experiencing the daily cycle of morning, noon, and night; the yearly cycle of the seasons; and changes in the weather contribute to children's ability to relate past experience to new situations and make predictions? How do you support children's experiences in nature?

INDICATOR 2: *The child speculates and demonstrates a beginning understanding of motivations and intentions, and what others are thinking.*

PLAYING HOUSE

"Honey, when's supper? The baby's hungry and me too."

"I'm making stew. It'll be ready in a minute. I just need to get the beans. You stir the pot and get the baby while I go get them."

Deshane, Keandra, and Corine are playing house on a grassy bank near the sandbox of their school yard. Keandra is the mom, Deshane the dad, and Corine the little baby. Each of the children is busy. Keandra has dug a little hole in the sand and is adding grass, twigs, and leaves to make their supper stew. Deshane is sweeping the floor of their home with an imaginary broom. Corine is curled up under a tree, taking her afternoon nap. As they play, the children talk together, alternately calling each other, "Mom," "Dad," "Baby," "Honey," or "Sweetie." As their dinnertime

approaches, Keandra makes the final additions to the stew, gathering some redbud pods from a nearby tree and carefully extracting the seeds to add to their meal.

SOME OF THE imaginative play children engage in outside is similar to, and often a continuation of, play that begins inside—and vice versa. This is to be expected, since frequently what they are trying to sort out are ideas that they are thinking about all the time. As children work to understand how the world works, the family system they are a part of provides them with the firsthand knowledge they need to reflect on social systems. As they seek to answer the questions, "Where do I belong?" and "Who am I?" issues of identity arise. Children need time to have conversations and engage in imaginary play around these questions.

Playing house or school and taking on roles of parents and community helpers are all ways to explore and understand the important relationships in their lives. Letting this play extend into the outdoors provides children with more time, space, and props to act out these roles. The outdoors offers a wealth of materials that are not available inside to incorporate into their play. The props and prompts of the natural world are open ended and adaptable in ways that the toy food, furniture, and kitchen utensils in the housekeeping center are not. Toy versions of real objects all bring a predefined meaning to children's play and, to some extent, tell them what to do. Outdoors, children may use sticks, acorns, and a nest made from leaves for similar home-making play. With these more ambiguous natural materials, the children have to be more creative to imbue the objects with a particular meaning. Because the objects are less defined, they require children's imaginations to work harder to decide on and communicate a definition.

Children come to school eager to share and explore ideas about their families. The concept of family is at the center of one's identity, especially as a young child. Deshane, Keandra, and Corine were motivated to portray their own experiences of family. To do this, they took on and played out the various roles they saw portrayed around them, at home, in their neighborhood, at their school, and in the media. Deshane and Keandra used pet names like "Honey" and "Sweetie" (which they may have heard at home) as they explored the relationships they were working to understand. Teachers can support children's conversations and imaginative play about family and community by providing time and space, both indoors and out. Another way to support children is to have conversations with them about roles and relationships that help them understand that families come in all shapes and sizes. This kind of exploration is critical if children are to come to understand families in all of their diversity: both their own families and those of others.

THE MILLIPEDE

"You have to watch out for millipedes. But they don't notice us and they don't sting us because we never bother them," says Shelby.

"We don't throw things at them. We don't bother them ever," agrees Quinn.

As two other children approach them, Shelby says, *"We found a millipede. Don't touch him. Maybe he's going to his home. Let's watch him."*

Quinn exclaims, *"Look! I think he's going into that hole."*

Quinn and Shelby discover a large millipede in the mulch on their play yard. Crouching down, they observe the millipede for several minutes as it makes its way across the mulch and under a bush. They talk together about how it moves. They notice its bright yellow legs and its brown body striped with bold yellow lines. When two other children come near, Shelby informs them of their discovery and asks them not to harm the insect. She and Quinn then resume their investigation, predicting where the millipede is going and watching it as it approaches a hole under the bush.

OUTDOOR ENVIRONMENTS are shared worlds where children coexist with all sorts of plants and animals, including insects. There is so much for them to learn about what lives in their particular environment and climate, as well as how living things come and go throughout the seasons. As children happen upon critters in the natural world, they have opportunities to learn from and about them. These encounters are exciting and can lead to important learning.

For children to know how to keep themselves safe, they need protocols on how to handle themselves around animals and insects, and then practice in doing so. Learning how to observe insects and animals from a safe distance—generally without touching them—protects both the animal and the children themselves. The power of such firsthand experience is invaluable and provides insight that children cannot gain any other way. Children who spend a lot of time outside and who have many experiences seeing and watching animals form a strong bond with the natural world. This makes it more likely that they will become good stewards of the environment.

Shelby and Quinn were demonstrating the confidence of true millipede experts. They crouched together comfortably, watching and chatting about the millipede, clearly feeling safe and secure in a situation where less experienced children might feel less comfortable. This ease was the result of knowledge they had accumulated over time. Their experience enabled them to recognize the millipede, anticipate how it would behave, and know that if they left it alone and just watched it, it would not hurt them. Knowing all this, they were not afraid of it, and could therefore take an active interest in what it was up to. They asked, "Where is it going?" "Why is it going under the bush?" "Is it hungry?" "Is it looking for food?" Using what they knew about their own needs and motivations, they applied this knowledge to the millipede and were able to reflect on what may be going on for the insect. It was less important that they were correct in the motivations and attitudes they attributed to the millipede than that they were engaged in the process of using what they knew and applying it to a new experience to see what they could figure out.

The Millipede is an example of the extensive world of living creatures and plant life underfoot and overhead outside. How does interacting with this living web support children's growing understanding of why living things do what they do? How do you support this type of learning?

INDICATOR 3: *The child uses play, representation, and discussion to process information and apply ideas.*

FROG HOUSE

"This is my frog house."

A group of children explore in the woods near their play yard with a teacher. Stopping at a mossy mound under a tree, they begin to look for insects and other critters. The teacher asks them what animals they think they might find in this habitat and Theo responds, "Frogs!" Because the group has been talking about the differences between frogs and toads and their habitats, another child interjects, "No! Toads!" The group discusses the two animals and their habitat requirements.

Returning to the play yard, Theo chooses a plastic frog from one of the outdoor toy bins. He takes it to a rock in a quiet spot and gathers moss, lichen, a single leaf, a small sheet of bark, and the tip of a cedar bough. With these materials, he spends thirty minutes constructing a home for his frog.

CHILDREN NEED OPPORTUNITIES to revisit and explore ideas multiple times, both through their conversations and their play. In this way, they test out and reflect on their understanding about how the world works. In the out-of-doors, children have an endless supply of materials from which to choose when building models and engaging in pretend play. Nature provides leaves, sticks, twigs, rocks, sand, cones, bark, seedpods, acorns, moss, lichen, and clay. Theo's project shows how children use materials such as these creatively in their pretend play to explore and answer questions such as "What is it like to be a frog?" Theo used a wide variety of natural objects, making fine distinctions and selecting just the right ones to have the effect he wanted. Encouraging children to explore and use materials and readily available loose parts in open-ended and original ways expands the breadth and complexity of their thinking.

Theo was very interested in what he was learning about animal habitats. He was processing the idea that different animals need different conditions to live. The walk in the woods offered him an opportunity to compare different habitats and speculate about what animal might be living there. Looking closely, he noticed that the plants and rocks in each habitat varied according to where there was sun or shade and where it was moist or dry. He remembered and applied the information he absorbed on the walk to the miniature world he built when he returned to the school yard.

Making this transference requires reflection, judgment, motivation, and focused effort. This kind of hands-on representation of firsthand learning is very satisfying to children. It provides an effective way for them to sort through and think about complex information. Allowing adequate time and space for children to initiate activities in which they can represent what they think they know and what they are wondering about leads to higher-level thinking.

OAK APPLE GALL

"It's a lime. Look, it has a stem."
  "No, it's too soft."
  "It's squishy. It's lumpy!"
  "It is light as a feather!"
  "What's inside?"

The children are on an expedition to a local state park. They follow a trail that takes them through a field, along a gentle river, and through a stand of pine and oak trees. Along the way they make many discoveries. They find fiddlehead ferns emerging from the ground, which they excitedly recognize and name from a book they read at school. They spot painted turtles sunning themselves on logs. They find shrubs of native azalea filling the forest with a pale pink light. They discover insects under bark and they stop to consider the cause of a loud eerie creaking sound they hear in the woods each time the wind blows. Gabriel finds a round, green, fruitlike object along the path.

He picks it up by the stem and takes a closer look. Just then, Rowan finds a larger one. While the two boys begin to compare what they have found, other children begin to notice similar objects scattered all along the path. The children gather in a group with their teacher and talk about what they have found.

THIS STORY illustrates the rich dialogue teachers can foster between direct exploration of the outdoors and information available to children in books and other sources. The children were using the outdoors as a field laboratory, responding to the things they found by applying their prior experience and knowledge. Their knowledge of the fiddlehead ferns that came from the book

at school made them feel as if they found an old friend when they saw the fiddleheads in the field. Such an experience of discovery and recognition is powerful and builds children's confidence in their own ability to know. The children in this story expressed this confidence by naming the place. "Look," they said, "this is "Fiddle Head Field."

Print media such as books, posters, and diagrams, and items in other indoor centers can be meaningfully linked to children's outdoor learning. Teachers need to continually add and highlight resources indoors in response to children's interests, questions, and the seasonal changes, and as preparation for upcoming activities. It is likely that the children in this story returned to their classroom and looked for images to help identify and explain the strange round objects they found on the forest floor. Supporting children's curiosity about particular topics, and helping them process information about events and ideas they may be exploring outside is a key role of teachers. It is less important initially that the children know that what they found were oak apple galls than that they have the opportunity and the resources to cultivate their wonder about them.

Even though the children and their teacher spent ten minutes investigating, describing, and asking questions about their find, it is important to note that at the end of this rich process, the children still did not know what the strange fruit was. They left with their curiosity intact and motivated to check back on their next visit to see if the green balls are still there and to look for more clues about what they might be. The children's curiosity will fuel further investigation using books and tools available to them back at school. They will tell their story to others as a way of reflecting on what they saw and developing their understanding. The drawing on this page shows one four-year-old's representation of the fibrous material he saw inside the oak apple gall. It is a vivid example of how children work to make sense of the mysteries and questions they encounter as they investigate the natural world around them. In these ways, their inquiry process continues beyond the actual event.

What is the role of the various loose parts featured in these two stories (the plastic frog, the moss, and the apple gall) in helping the children process information as they play? What loose parts are available outdoors for the children you teach?

You can promote reflection, interpretation, and application by encouraging children to revisit experiences and questions and, at the same time, hold off on the temptation to provide them with the "right answer." Giving them the answer stops this valuable process. This standard recognizes an important principle: having the answer is less important than engaging fully in the process of wondering and figuring things out. Children need repeated practice with the process of reflecting, interpreting, and applying their experience to become good problem solvers.

Further Reflection

How might applying the reflection, interpretation, and application standard affect your teaching outdoors?

The stories in this chapter show how the patterns, cycles, and repetitions of the natural world help children develop a conceptual framework of how the world works. By visiting and revisiting related and increasingly familiar events and phenomena, children order and structure their understanding. Encounters with nature offer children exactly the kind of concrete hands-on experiences they need as learners at this stage in their development. "This is an age where . . . learning goes from the hand to the head, not the other way around" (Wood 1997, 33). Children explore with their whole bodies, using all of their senses. Their everyday real-life activities become the springboard for reflection as they sift through their experience thinking about what they are seeing, interpreting what happens, and applying what they know as they act on their environment.

Life is the art of drawing without an eraser.

JOHN GARDNER

8

Flexibility and Resilience Standard

RESILIENCE IS A TERM best understood from life experience. It may be thought of as the ability to bounce back from difficulties or recover quickly from challenging incidents and keep moving forward. Or, resilience may be identified as a capacity to grow and thrive in spite of adverse circumstances. It is often recognized in an individual as a characteristic that enables one to navigate through stressful periods while maintaining self-confidence and a sense of optimism. All of these views of resilience are compatible with, and help teachers understand, this standard in action as it relates to young children.

The relationship between flexibility and early childhood development, however, is perhaps less readily understood. What is meant by flexibility as an approach to learning? Flexibility is the capacity children exhibit that allows them to approach a problem with openness and conviction. Flexibility encompasses the idea that numerous solutions to a problem may exist and that the child is going to find one! It also refers to a plasticity of thought, perspective, and process. With regard to the standard, it means that children are able to see and experiment with multiple approaches. Rather than trying only one previously successful approach to a problem, for example, and then giving up if it does not work, they regroup and try again. When children move beyond the safety of a method they have generalized from prior learning and, instead, try another way, they exhibit the ethic this standard encompasses.

Dance provides an analogy for thinking about the value of flexibility as a powerful approach to learning. Accomplished dancers can bend, change direction, move easily up and down, maintain balance, and stretch, all with confidence and a sense of where they are in space. Similarly, children are most powerful when they are able to use their minds with flexibility—bending, stretching, changing direction, and trying new ways of looking at and solving problems.

Overview

Why is the flexibility and resilience standard important for healthy child development?

Children exhibit a great deal of variance in their ability to manage adversity and rebound from defeat and challenge. Some children seem more able than others to regroup and "land on their feet" after a disappointment or failure. These children are able to maintain or recover a positive attitude and learn from each experience. They tend to approach tasks and challenges with greater willingness to try different approaches and make changes or course corrections as they work. Children who are less buoyant, less quick to recover, and more tentative about making mistakes tend to be more restricted in their ability to learn from experience. They also tend to be more rigid in their approach to a new task. They are less able to fine-tune their approach or make changes that may be necessary as they work through a problem. As a result, over time, they are likely to become less and less motivated to attempt challenging tasks.

Resilience is the ability to recover or rebound quickly in the face of defeat, whereas flexibility is the accompanying ability to make corrections or changes in one's approach when working through a problem. The more flexible children are in their thinking and interactions, the more creative and inventive they can be as they confront new questions, problems, and information. Flexibility and resilience enhance children's development in all areas.

Together, flexibility and resilience are approaches to learning and experience that matter a great deal throughout children's lives. They affect not only the quality of their learning but the level of stress children may experience in the process and how they feel about themselves. Teachers play a key role in helping children sustain flexibility and develop resilience over time, both through their own modeling and interaction with the children and through the physical environment and activities they provide.

You can support children's flexibility and resilience in a number of ways. Primary among these are creating a strong personal relationship with each child and nurturing positive interactions between the children themselves. It is also important to create a climate of support and acceptance in which children have opportunities to make mistakes and learn from them. Designing and provisioning the environment in a way that encourages children to make choices and pursue their own personal goals and interests best accomplishes this. Providing such a setting gives children opportunities to practice independence and become increasingly confident.

This discussion illustrates how flexibility is linked to resilience. Children who readily apply multiple strategies to a problem and have the confidence to believe in their ability to find a solution are more likely to be able to cope with setbacks. Such children show optimism, purpose, and conviction. Children who approach a learning challenge or task with an openness to try multiple approaches and think flexibly about solutions demonstrate the resilience needed to push through difficulties and bounce back. These children are more likely to overcome obstacles and pursue problems until they reach a solution. Flexibility and resilience are strongly linked in their impact on approaches to problem solving and learning. This standard reminds teachers as they plan activities, design their spaces, and interact with children to attend to ways to help children practice flexibility to promote the development of resilience.

Pragmatic View

How do states and national early childhood organizations classify flexibility and resilience?

In looking at early learning standards across the nation, little emphasis is placed on flexibility and resilience as important attributes of young learners. When flexibility shows up in state standards, it is alternately paired with inventiveness, risk taking, or problem solving. While resilience is generally not articulated in early learning standards, it is a powerful predictor of children's lifelong learning habits because it is deeply tied to children's belief in themselves. It is a measure of their optimism about life and the possibilities they believe it holds for them.

Resilience is hard to operationalize because it is a global quality, the sum of a child's approaches and attitudes and feelings of hope and confidence. Resilience builds in classrooms where children are encouraged to learn from both their successes and their failures and when mistakes are valued as a fundamental part of the learning process. With the right educational approach and classroom climate, children can often learn more from their mistakes than from their successes. If children are taught to examine and learn from their failures and mistakes without negative impact to their self-esteem, they become increasingly able to try again while maintaining a positive attitude. When these children experience a setback, they are more likely to recover quickly. This is resilience in action.

We have paired flexibility and resilience here to emphasize the critical link that exists between them. Flexibility is an important skill in the context of intellectual growth and children's thinking. But, importantly, it also has a social-emotional component that strongly affects children's healthy growth and development of their confidence, independence, and sense of well-being. Flexibility and resilience address children's capacity to ask critical questions and know how to proceed when they are stuck, while at the same time continuing to believe in themselves and their abilities.

Applied View

What are the observable behaviors or indicators that demonstrate children engaging with the flexibility and resilience standard?

When children are feeling confident and in charge, it is often expressed in how they move their bodies; the expressions on their faces; and their stance as they talk, work, and play with others. It is easy to imagine what children look like when they feel ownership and control over a project. A picture comes immediately to mind of children trying and succeeding at a difficult task. Children experiencing ownership and accomplishment exude a sense of forward movement and "standing tall" that feels good to them and to the observer. We have written the indicators below to encompass this recognizable quality teachers can look for as they observe children working and playing. Recognizing these indicators in action requires that teachers be attentive and observant and willing to use their own perceptions and professional judgment as tools for assessment.

We have synthesized from the observable behaviors articulated in the various state standards four representative indicators of flexibility and resilience for three- to five-year-olds:

1. The child demonstrates a sense of optimism, ownership, and a realistic sense of personal control.

2. The child is willing to attempt tasks that previously were difficult.

3. The child shows a growing ability to control impulses, accepting and adjusting to unplanned, unwanted, and unexpected events or outcomes.

4. The child demonstrates comfort with open-ended questions and problems.

Experiencing the Flexibility and Resilience Standard in the Outdoors

INDICATOR 1: *The child demonstrates a sense of optimism, ownership, and a realistic sense of personal control.*

TRAFFIC COP

"Stop! I blow my whistle and someone stops! All of them don't stop. She don't stop and he don't stop. They think it's funny."

Katharine has a bright yellow whistle. She goes to the curve of the trike path and watches several children as they ride by. When the next rider approaches, she blows her whistle, but the child continues on around the corner. She turns to watch him go, and then tries again with the next rider, this time extending her arm straight out in front of her as she blows her whistle. Still the child does not stop. As she sees the next trike coming around the corner, she steps out onto the path, extends her arm, blows her whistle, and shouts, "Stop!" This time the child stops. She smiles at Katharine and asks, "Are you the police officer?"

YOUNG CHILDREN are intensely interested in opportunities to explore and act out the issues, problems, and experiences of their daily lives. This is the major vehicle available to them to understand their world. Topics such as community life, family life, and transportation are compelling ones that children often investigate through dramatic play. The outdoors is particularly conducive to this kind of play. Its open-ended materials support children's imaginations. Its larger spaces make it possible for children to create multiple pretend shops, offices, and homes, and develop routes between them.

These activities allow children to explore the connections and relationships between various community resources as well as their own family life. It gives them a chance to think about what a community needs to function. Props such as hats, stop signs, and vehicles can help children explore different roles and think about what these people actually do by "doing it." This kind of play is fascinating to children, who are particularly curious about the adults they see and meet in their own communities. Complex communities can take shape on play yards over a period of days or weeks as children refine and add to their ideas and rearrange the space.

Katharine was interested in the role of being a traffic cop and especially in the power associated with this role. Using her bright yellow whistle, she wanted to direct traffic on the trike path and have children stop at her command. Though persistent and determined, she nonetheless discovered that this work was more complicated than she anticipated. Some children were eager to listen and cooperate while others rode right by without stopping or acknowledging her. Katharine, however, did not give up when her first attempts to stop the traffic were ignored. Instead, she altered her tactics several times, changing her approach and her position until she found a combination that got the result she wanted. What she found out was that the yellow whistle could not work the magic by itself. It did not, in and of itself, have the power to make the other children cooperate with her idea. It was only by being flexible and willing to experiment with a number of different approaches that she was able to discover what it took to elicit the collaboration and participation of the other children.

CLAY ROSES

"Want me to teach you how to make a rose? We'll start with the small one. Then you score it."

"Molly, look!"

"Good! Do you want a stem on it?"

"Okay."

"Well, stems are easy. Roll a small snake. Look, this one can be yours. Want a leaf on it? Do you want to draw the triangle for the stem or do you want me to do it? Here's your leaf!"

Several children are sitting outside at a picnic table. The space has been set up with a variety of tools and materials for working with clay. There are bins with varied clay tools for rolling, cutting, stamping, and drawing. As well as a large bag of clay, there is a container of water and another container of slip (a mixture of clay and water used for cementing pieces together). In addition,

there are objects for imprinting textures, paddles for smoothing edges, and a string with handles that children can use to cut more slabs of clay as they need them. At the side are Masonite boards the children use to transport their completed projects safely inside to dry before they are fired.

Molly makes a clay rose. She notices that Amelia, who is a year older, is watching her as she works. Molly offers to teach Amelia to make her own rose. Molly models and explains each step of the process, helping Amelia when she gets stuck. With Molly's assistance, Amelia makes a rose. As soon as they finish, Amelia reaches for more clay and begins again. She makes a new rose, this time completely on her own. Setting it carefully on a Masonite board, she goes on to make several more.

CHILDREN BENEFIT from having lots of opportunities to work with and express themselves through the arts. Providing arts experiences outside as well as inside encourages several wonderful things to happen. Bringing arts materials outside gives children more time and more exposure to art as a means of self-expression, a source of sensory experience, and a way to improve fine-motor development and enhance creativity. It gives children double the time to explore materials and learn about them.

Another benefit is that children have the opportunity to study and incorporate elements of the outdoors into their work. They may represent what they are seeing or they may incorporate natural materials into the work itself. And there is an added benefit for teachers: it is easier and less stressful for children and teachers to work with and clean up messy materials like clay outside than in!

Molly had been perfecting her ability to make clay roses for a number of days. This was both a creative and a complex task she initiated on her own. What enabled Molly to approach this difficult work with the confidence and flexibility apparent in the story? First, her teacher created a climate that encouraged and rewarded children for taking different approaches to solving problems, trying new things, experimenting, and learning from their mistakes. As a result of this supportive climate, the children believed that they could "do anything they put their minds to."

This resilient and optimistic attitude, combined with access to open-ended materials such as clay, enabled Molly to experiment and persist at her self-selected task for many days in a row. She demonstrated the ownership she felt for her idea by generously offering to share her technique and skills with another child. She modeled each step of the process for Amelia, matching her explanation to Amelia's responses, questions, and needs. Molly watched and listened attentively. She showed great flexibility of thought as a teacher, fine-tuning and individualizing her presentation at each step along the way. A measure of her accomplishment is seen in the independence Amelia displayed when she took the skills she learned from Molly and confidently applied them on her own. She then went on to make several more roses completely on her own.

In Clay Roses, the teacher's setup, planning, and provisioning of the space are critical factors in Molly's ability to take on the role of teacher. How might you set up an activity outdoors that would enable children to take this same kind of ownership of their work and feel this same sense of personal control?

THE SANDBOX

"Can you please stop doing that to him? Right now!"

Carrie, Britton, and Seth are playing together in the sandbox. They fill a big plastic bucket and then continue to pile sand on top, mounding it above the rim of the bucket. They pack the sand as they work to form a pyramid shape. All three children are tightly focused on their task and seem not to be paying attention to the activities around them. George, an older youngster who has not been involved in the play, comes up behind Seth and dumps a handful of sand on his shoulder. When Seth does not respond, George does it again, this time spilling sand down Seth's collar. Although Seth himself still does

not react, Britton very clearly objects. She demands that George stop immediately. "Can you please stop doing that to him? Right now!" George does stop, looks at her, hesitates, then carefully brushes the sand from Seth's shoulder.

THE OUTDOORS provides children with many opportunities to interact and practice social skills. Outdoors, children tend to have more freedom to move about and interact together in unscripted ways. As a result, they are constantly practicing conflict resolution, negotiation, sharing, turn taking, and other important social skills. Children acquire these skills in context; they learn them by practicing them. This makes the outdoors both an opportunity and a challenge. Teachers must be attentive to the many different interactions taking place all around the school yard. They must be aware of the needs and skills of the individual children. They must also be able to assess, in the moment, whether and how to be involved when a difficulty or social conflict occurs. Since the goal is for children to become increasingly competent socially and able to solve problems with each other, teachers must allow them to practice and develop the interpersonal skills they have. The outdoors, with its spacious feeling, spontaneous events, and diverse choices offers constant opportunities for children to practice and polish these important skills.

George evidently wanted to join the children in the sandbox, but did not seem to know how to enter their play. As sometimes happens in a situation where a child has limited social skills, George initially made contact in a way that did not feel good to the other children. He lacked the repertoire of skills needed to know what to say and how to act to be able to join the group to be part of the sand play. In some settings, his slightly aggressive action toward Seth would have isolated him further from the group.

Often the children in a group also lack the skills and experiences to respond productively when a playmate is seeking attention in a negative way. Under these circumstances, they may resort to ostracizing or turning their backs on the child who has made the inappropriate overture. However, when children have real-world practice interacting and negotiating with each other as an integral part of their play, they develop the skills to help each other repair such awkward encounters. In this story, Britton addressed George directly, clearly communicating to him that he needed to behave differently to be included in their play. By doing so, she gave him an opening to redress his mistake. George not only stopped what he was doing but also tried to make amends by cleaning the sand off of Seth's shoulder. His effort to make things right gained him entry into the group.

Britton stood up for Seth, who was not yet able to stand up for himself. Many young children like Britton exhibit strong empathy for their peers as well as a conviction around what is right and wrong. In protecting Seth's rights, she was modeling how to do the right thing in a democratic classroom. She spoke with determination, courage, and confidence. Being a leader and advocating for others involves a lot of skill. It also requires a lot of practice. Children are able to develop this ability when they believe in themselves and are confident and flexible enough to try different approaches in different situations. They are more able to take on this important and difficult work when they have a teacher who is observant, involved, and ready to step in when help is needed. In this case, George, Seth, and Britton's teacher was wise enough to give them the opportunity to try to solve this social situation independently using the communication tools and skills modeled and promoted over the course of the year.

HAND CLEANING

"I can do that!"

As part of an extended study about food, farms, and farm animals, a local farmer has been invited to bring a goat and her two goat kids to school for a day. It is a sunny March morning and during their outdoor time, the children have an opportunity to visit with the mama goat and her two babies. Their teachers have made a pen with movable fencing for the goats during their visit.

Before heading outside, the teachers review with the children the importance of using quiet voices and gentle movements to keep both the goats and themselves safe. They offer the children the option of observing the goats from outside the pen or coming inside, in small groups with a teacher, to take a closer look. Some children choose a vantage point outside the pen and watch the babies nurse, jump, and frolic. Some go inside to hold the baby goats gently on their laps and pet them.

As the children leave the fenced area following these activities, the teacher gives them an individual reminder to stop at the hand-cleaning station, which she has conveniently set up right outside the gate on top of a barrel. As Kevin and Deirdre take their turns at the station, Deirdre, who is younger, stops a moment and watches Kevin pump the sanitizing solution onto his hands. After observing what to do, she thinks, "I can do that!" and steps forward, confidently following suit. She pumps the soap onto her hands, rubs them vigorously together, and inspects the result before she heads off to play.

THE OUTDOORS brings children close to the ongoing systems of plant and animal life around them. They may glimpse indigenous animals that live in their geographic area and have a chance to observe their appearance and behavior. Importantly, children can also learn about farm animals involved in food production and the farm economy of their community. Teachers often think of field trips to farms as the only way for this to happen. Increasingly, schools are recognizing the value for children in having regular contact with animals. Local farmers are often eager partners in making this happen by bringing animals to schools.

Learning about and caring for animals teaches children empathy and responsibility and gives them a beginning understanding of where their food comes from. Understanding where food comes from is a critical concept that is missing from many children's understanding of the world—and increasingly from that of adults as well. Creative teachers, working with their local licensing agencies, are finding ways to meet health and safety regulations so that children can continue to have important hands-on experiences with animals. These experiences enable children to explore and inquire about the fundamental connections that underlie their lives. Where does milk come from? How is cheese made? Do chickens lay eggs? How do they do that? How do fruits and vegetables grow? How does wheat get turned into bread? Knowing where food comes from is basic information everyone should have. You have a unique opportunity to equip children with the understanding, information, and connection they need to make good decisions about managing and conserving the environment when they become adults.

Deirdre knew she was expected to wash her hands after playing with the baby goats. She was used to washing her hands with soap and water inside, and with daily practice had become very competent at doing this independently. Outside, the task was altered and as a result was potentially more difficult for her. Her teacher, understanding the importance of the hand-cleaning routine, placed a hand-cleaning station right outside the animal pen. This made it possible for everyone to take care of cleaning their hands immediately after handling the animals, and enabled her to monitor the children as they did so. Deirdre went right up to the barrel and watched Kevin closely to see how he rubbed the sanitizer thoroughly between each of his fingers and continued rubbing until his hands were dry. Deirdre's confidence, buoyed by the modeling Kevin provided, helped her know just what to do, even though this was a brand new and unfamiliar task for her.

The Hand Cleaning story is a vivid example of how many of the early learning standards apply equally to both teachers and children. How did this teacher demonstrate flexibility in meeting important health requirements? What are the benefits to the children of their teacher's approach to the problem? How do you support children's learning while maintaining health requirements outdoors?

INDICATOR 3: *The child shows a growing ability to control impulses, accepting and adjusting to unplanned, unwanted, and unexpected events or outcomes.*

THE ALONE PLACE

Gabriel decides to take a break.

It is, as always, a busy day on the play yard. Some children are digging in the sand area, building canals and dams while others are working in the garden, setting out the pea plants they started from seed several weeks earlier in cups indoors. Farther down the hill, several boys and girls are riding trikes, wearing firefighter hats, and racing to a pretend fire, using their loud voices as sirens.

Gabriel has been playing a running game with several friends, darting from one end of the play yard to the other. Suddenly he steps out of the fast-paced activity and moves to the hammock, a designated "alone space" that is always available for individual children when they are outside. Leaning into the side of the hammock, he takes a few breaths and watches the busy activity all around him. After a few quiet moments, he sighs, skips off, and rejoins the fast-paced action of the other children.

THE OUTDOORS is a characteristically busy, active place. Within it, children need a safe space where they can elect to take a break as they navigate their work and play. The hammock in this story, for example, offers a spot for a quick respite. Children use it in many ways. Like Gabriel, they may use it to catch their breath. They have learned to visit it for longer breaks as a place to recover their equilibrium when their feelings have been hurt or if they feel overwhelmed. It is an important safe zone that children can use as they learn to manage and control their impulses. They can remove themselves and regroup when they are feeling angry, hurt, or volatile. It is also a place from which to observe play when they are not yet ready to join in—a place to be shy and scope out what is happening and plan how best to enter a game or activity of interest.

Additionally, visiting a set-aside alone spot can provide children with a means of communicating to their friends that something has occurred that is not feeling okay. When alone spaces like the hammock include a swinging motion, they can be particularly effective in helping children restore their sensory systems to better balance.

Gabriel was actually having a good time participating in the running game with his friends. He was running nonstop, darting in and out on his way from one end of the play yard to the other. This kind of play requires a lot of physical energy and concentration. At a certain point, he momentarily ran out of gas. When this happened, he used the alone space as a temporary retreat where he could catch his breath and rest for a moment. The alone space functioned both as an indicator to his friends that he wanted a break and as a place for him to reorganize himself while still watching the action. In planning and equipping outdoor learning environments for children, it is important that teachers take all the information they have about children's physical, social-emotional, language, creative, and cognitive needs and apply it to the spaces and places they design.

TO CATCH A LEAF

"I'm going to catch one!"

It is a breezy day in late autumn. Most of the leaves of the hardwood trees have changed colors and fallen to the ground, carpeting the play yard floor with crisp and crunch. Today, as the wind ruffles the remaining leaves up above in the trees, some of them are coaxed free from the fragile hold on their branches. They drift down through the air, playfully dancing as they make the journey to the ground.

   Phin watches their movement. His gaze follows them, from one leaf to the other, as he sees them falling all around him. After watching for a few moments, he exclaims aloud, "I'm going to catch one!" Hands outstretched, he races across the yard toward several leaves that are twisting and turning in the air, but he is unable to grasp them as they make their way to the ground. He then spies more leaves falling and rushes off in another direction, racing to reach and catch the leaves before they hit the ground.

After many tries over fifteen minutes or so, a smile still on his face, Phin walks up to a pile of leaves near the edge of the play yard. Reaching down, he grabs an enormous armful and tosses them up in the air, letting them cascade down around his head and shoulders and into his hands.

In both of these stories, The Alone Place and To Catch a Leaf, the boys take the initiative to resolve their own difficulties without any direct help from a teacher. How did their teachers' planning and behavior contribute to the boys' ability to do this on their own? When have you chosen to wait and observe rather than intervene?

SO MANY of the activities that engage children outdoors are unplanned, spontaneous experiences that are composed in the moment. They arise directly from the materials at hand and the qualities of those materials, from what is happening in the moment and from how that calls to the individual child. Teachers feel responsible for providing learning experiences for children. Children, however, can be trusted to find valuable, meaningful learning encounters on their own. They are already equipped with the tools that fuel meaningful learning. They are curious, inquisitive, motivated, and eager to explore. These qualities act as drivers moving them to just the right place at just the right time to have encounters saturated with meaning. This is especially true in the outdoors where so many lessons are waiting to be delved into by children.

One of the great challenges confronting teachers is where to put their energies so that these lessons will unfold. Sometimes this involves stepping back and giving children the space to create moments of learning for themselves. Watching these lessons unfold, you can judge when to provide questions, support, additional materials, and extensions—or when to just observe.

Phin was engaged in a challenging activity. As the leaves fell from the trees, the wind moved them in unexpected ways, making it difficult for him to catch them before they hit the ground. Although he adjusted his strategy a number of times—running faster, using both hands, following leaves while they were still very high up in the air—he was still unable to meet his goal of catching one in his hand. Yet his attitude remained playful, optimistic, and determined. He approached each try as a fresh opportunity. After repeated attempts, he gleefully restructured the entire activity to experience the success he wanted. Grabbing an armful of leaves and tossing them into the air, he guaranteed that he could at last catch a leaf!

SUN STUDY

"I'm making sparkle hands. You rub them in the sand. You make sure they have sparkles."

Miranda is running with a friend. She is perspiring in the hot sun. She wipes her face with her hand and climbs into the shaded sandbox. She sits by herself, the sun at her back. Staring into space, she idly runs her hands through the cool sand, feeling the texture and sifting the grains. She lifts her hands, now coated with sand, in front of her face and looks at them. Her expression changes to one of intent interest. Rotating her hands slowly, she moves them one way and then another, exploring this glittering transformation.

OUTDOORS children have powerful encounters with light and dark, reflections, shadows, and the rich colors of nature. They are able to have firsthand experiences with the characteristics and behavior of natural light and what it reveals, experiences that are rarely available inside. Outdoors, they observe and play with shadows. They see what happens to sunlight when it passes through a colored object like a petal or a leaf. Children study reflections in raindrops and puddles, and see what light does when it plays on water, sand, and other surfaces. They experience how the quality of light changes on sunny and cloudy days. They follow sunbeams through the branches of trees. They watch the light and the shadows change throughout the course of the day. The value of this incidental learning is hard to measure but important to understand. Experiencing light and how it interacts with objects has aesthetic value and also creates a beginning scientific framework for children's thinking.

Miranda became hot and uncomfortable in the full sun of her school yard. On her own, she sought out a shaded place that she knew from experience would be cooler and more comfortable for her. Once there, she became engaged with an unplanned event. She poked her sweaty hands into the cool sand and found that when she pulled them out, they were covered with a fine coating of crystals. When she held her hands out in front of her to look at them more carefully, the sunlight streaming over her shoulder reflected off her hands and lit up her face. Some of the individual grains of sand acted as mirrors and sparkled; others acted as prisms breaking the light into its many different colors. Miranda was intrigued by this event and spent several minutes wondering, "What is going on here?" By investigating what she saw, and talking aloud to herself about it, she pondered this mysterious and unexpected interaction.

CLOUD STUDY

"Look up there! Those white clouds are going to turn dark. The clouds will turn gray, dark gray, and I think it's going to rain while we're sleeping tonight and get really, really dark and then it will be all colored clouds."

It is a sunny day with big puffy white clouds in the sky. Sophia, Jackson, and Mira lie on the cement porch next to the building and chat about a game they have been playing with the balls. Their bodies are relaxed and they sprawl comfortably across the pavement, using the balls as pillows. When a passing cloud suddenly shadows the sun, their bodies tense, they stop talking, and look up at the sky.

WEATHER CHANGES are full of drama for children to observe and think about. Like adults, children are interested in the weather. It commands their attention and invites speculation about what is going on and what will happen next. Watching the weather connects children to the cycles of the day and year, introducing them to recurring patterns and events and prompting myriad questions. Having the time to watch clouds drift in the sky, follow the wind through a garden, watch puddles accumulate when it rains, and observe that water runs downhill are all benefits children glean from spending unscheduled time outside. Knowledge of natural systems builds gradually over time as children notice, observe, speculate, and test out their own open-ended questions about the world they see, smell, hear, and touch.

Sophia, Jackson, and Mira participated earlier in the day in a tornado drill in which clouds, wind, and storm movements were discussed. Later, they connected what they saw in the sky with their earlier classroom discussion about signs of possible tornado activity. Together they watched the sky, noticing and pointing out details of cloud shape and color. They commented on the speed and direction in which the clouds were moving and compared that to the speed of the wind. They made inferences and predictions about a coming

In both of these stories, Sun Study and Cloud Study, the children are pondering big ideas. The outdoors is full of mysteries and open-ended questions to which not all the answers are known. In what ways can you support children as they pursue their ongoing process of inquiry and discovery?

change in the weather. They took information acquired in their classroom work and applied it to their firsthand observations outside.

There is a rich partnership between formal curriculum and children's self-directed activities. Hands-on and firsthand experiences allow children to construct their own knowledge and connect what they are taught by adults to their own discoveries in the real world. This story shows how systematically children test out and apply the things they've heard to the experiences that follow, continually extending and refining their understanding. By providing time and a rich outdoor environment, teachers support children's natural propensity to make sense of the world around them.

Further Reflection

How might applying the flexibility and resilience standard affect your teaching outdoors?

The outdoors is a place of continuous change where many real stories are unfolding at the same time. Leaves are falling, snow is melting, sunbeams are bouncing, worms are emerging from the ground, and on and on. By simply being outside, children come to understand that interesting things are always at hand and that nature's recurring patterns are reliable and predictable. They come to know that events they miss seeing today may recur tomorrow, or that some other exciting event may come along to captivate their interest. The outdoors encourages children to be flexible by offering them variety and the experience of change.

Phin, chasing leaves, was invited to run fast and then slow down, to turn this way and then that way, depending on how the wind was blowing and the weight and shape of the leaf. And when Phin failed to catch a leaf, he knew that a different leaf would soon come along and he would have another chance. When none of his strategies worked, the materials were at hand for him to remake his experience into one that did meet his goal.

When children are invited to do so many different things in so many different ways, they will almost always find some that they both enjoy and are good at. This flexible quality of the outdoors makes it a place of second chances, a place where it is difficult for children to fail. An environment that is so knowable, interesting, and dependable supports children's optimism, imagination, and resilience. In such an environment, children have the chance to move on to new activities, equally engaging, interesting, or challenging, as they need to. The natural world thus inspires confidence, cultivates optimism, and supports the development of resilience.

The play space—trees, shrubs, paths, hidings, climbings—is a visible, structured entity . . .
PAUL SHEPARD

Structuring Outdoor Learning: The Environment and the Teacher

THROUGHOUT THIS BOOK, we have used standards and indicators as a lens for looking at and analyzing children's experiences outside. The stories and the settings in which they unfold are varied. They offer examples of the kinds of rich experiences children can have in thoughtful outdoor settings, whether in cities or in the countryside, in a large center or a small in-home child care. The children in the stories come from diverse cultural and socioeconomic backgrounds, have various abilities and needs, and bring to their experiences unique expectations and sensibilities. Their diversity is evident in the scope of what captivates and engages their attention. The stories show how the environment answers their interests and needs and, in particular, how the natural world is unique in its ability to respond to the enormous depth with which young children engage. These stories reveal a dialogue continually unfolding between the environment, each child, and the teacher. This three-way conversation is the structure that supports the powerful learning that happens outdoors for children.

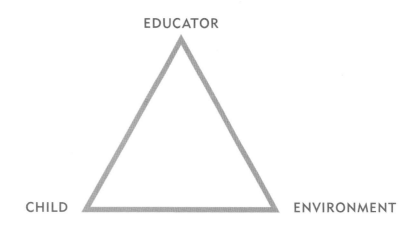

The stories recount and document the largely unexplored role of children learning in the outdoors. They portray the children's actions, what they are saying, and how they are making meaning from powerful firsthand experiences. The descriptions and reflections provide insights into how the environment supports children's growth and development. The images show the various environments in which the stories take place; sometimes they include the teachers who work with the children. The stories and images focus on the children's role within their own learning process and document how they use the environment.

This chapter rounds out the picture by focusing on how the environment and teachers work in partnership, sharing the role of providing outdoor learning experiences for children. It examines both the qualities and characteristics of the environment and the attitudes, skills, and understandings needed to participate effectively in children's outdoor learning. This chapter revisits the stories with a tight focus on the environment and the educator. It identifies the elements each brings to support healthy childhood development as delineated by the early learning standards. By reflecting on the stories, you, as the teacher, can better understand your role in the dialogue between you, the environment, and the children you teach.

Natural environments offer a uniquely rich setting with which to interact and explore. The ideas children confront outside are profound and a part of the conceptual fabric that underpins our world. Concepts of physics, biology, botany, and geology, for example, are all accessible to children daily during outdoor play. In the outdoors, children are immersed in interconnected systems and big ideas. This makes the outdoors an ideal place for children to practice and apply their approaches to learning.

Nature is thus a key player in meeting early learning standards. Where else can children lie on their backs and wonder why clouds move across the sky? Where else can they observe the transformation of a green tree into a golden one during the fall, and then watch it drop its leaves to the ground one by one? Where else can children discover where frogs lay their eggs, or come upon a dead bird and wonder what happens when an animal or a person dies? Where else can they discover ice in a bucket that yesterday held water? Many of the things that happen outside for children simply cannot happen anywhere else. These mysteries and transformations engage children by allowing them to apply the standards to powerful and meaningful real-life events. The stories in this book document events and experiences that cannot be duplicated inside.

Interaction with the natural environment has a dynamic quality. In the natural world every action is an opportunity to learn about cause and effect and how things work. Here children have an ongoing experience applying and practicing their approaches to learning, constantly modifying and refining the strategies they use. This ongoing dialogic process supports children in becoming more sophisticated as they learn from experience which approach to apply, when, and in what way. Children cannot be rushed through this process. It is not linear and cannot be closely controlled and directed. Your role in this process is to plan the environment and give children the time to explore it so that they are increasingly in charge of their own learning.

The Unique Role of the Teacher

You, like most educators, have come to teaching because you care about children and want to help them learn. You bring with you whatever tools you have accumulated along the way, from your experiences and upbringing, your own education, and the professional training you have pursued. You arrive hoping to use your tools and energy for the maximum benefit of the children in your care. You also come knowing that you are still learning and growing professionally. One of the benefits of working in this field is that you will always have the chance to do so. Planning for children's learning outside is full of challenges as well as possibilities for learning and growth. By recognizing and welcoming the potential the outdoors offers for professional development, you can advance your teaching practice in significant ways.

Outdoor learning for both children and teachers is all about process. In the outdoors, you see children thinking, reasoning, problem solving, risk taking, reflecting, interpreting, inventing, and persisting. In other words, you witness all the processes that are fundamental to learning how to learn. Because the outdoor environment readily involves children with materials and ideas, it encourages them to engage with this wide range of approaches to learning. In natural outdoor environments, all of the standards are naturally called into action, often without any direct instruction from the teacher. Knowing this to be the case, what then is your crucial role in outdoor learning?

Your role outside is qualitatively different from the one experienced in the indoor classroom. The outdoors asks you to make a shift and to focus primarily on observing, supporting, and extending learning. It requires you to focus less on content and product and more on children's process. Many teachers are trained to think of curricula in terms of content and skills, and to plan sequential activities to further those outcomes. The shift comes with the recognition that with appropriate provisioning, the outdoors comes with its content already in place. As described throughout this book, content is embedded in children's interactions outdoors with elements such as loose parts, changes, natural systems, and plant and animal life. With so much curriculum provided by the natural world, your role becomes one of observation and recognition, noticing what children are doing and learning, and then considering how to extend and support their explorations and play. The standards and indicators provide an important framework for thinking about and analyzing the work and play of children.

Without such a framework, it's possible to forget that playtime outside is prime learning time. While the conventional role of playground supervisor continues to be a very important one, your role outdoors extends beyond supervision and is really quite complex. To maximize opportunities for children's learning, you must be really "on" and "present." You need to observe, provision, document, question, analyze, extend, and engage with children in ways that actively support their learning. The standards and indicators help support this work by providing a framework for identifying and valuing the important learning that is taking place all around you.

This learning can be difficult to identify and understand because it follows the children's initiative and is encountered in dribs and drabs rather than as an orderly sequence. It is also hard to observe because children are pursuing independent paths and operating at different levels. The ensuing variety of movement, engagement, and content ensures that every child is engaged at an appropriate level. This setting requires you to practice higher-level thinking and engage directly with children and materials to understand their individual ideas and questions. Understanding the depth of the children's experiences is both a prerequisite and a reward for this kind of teaching.

Seen from this perspective, standards provide a useful road map for thinking about how children learn by cataloging the complex and varied ways they learn so you can recognize them in action. Once recognized, you can extend and help children refine the strategies and approaches they are using.

The stories show how often the children's approaches are supported and mirrored by their teachers' behavior. Of the many settings depicted in this book, children had the most meaningful experiences when teachers exhibited the same positive qualities and attitudes toward learning as the children. Curious, engaged teachers were surrounded by curious, engaged children. Teachers who modeled inquiry and open-ended questions were rewarded by children who bubbled over with questions of their own. When teachers demonstrated stick-to-itiveness, the children seemed to find it easier to engage and persist. Teachers who set up their environments to encourage choice and independence had the most independent, confident children. You can see that the behaviors and the attitudes of the teacher are integral to the quality of the experience children have. The depth and degree to which children engage with the standards is strongly influenced by the approach taken by their teacher.

The rest of this chapter takes a closer look at some of the discrete skills and behaviors teachers exhibit that are relevant specifically to supporting outdoor learning: provisioning, observing and reflecting, relationship building, and planning and restructuring. It also looks at specific elements of the natural environment that contribute powerfully to children's learning: loose parts, changes, natural systems, and plant and animal life. Both teachers and the environment bring their own contribution to the plentiful learning environment outdoors. It is when you operate as a partner with the environment that children can best engage and find that "just right fit" where they feel comfortable and competent.

The Role of Materials and Loose Parts

Children express themselves and explore the world importantly through the manipulation of objects. They need many opportunities to handle, arrange, sort, classify, build, and imagine, using the things around them. The more numerous and more varied the materials at hand, the more the child's imagination has to work with. Simon Nicholson formulated the theory of loose parts saying, "In any environment, both the degree of inventiveness and creativity and the possibility of discovery are directly proportional to the number and kind of variables in it" (1971). One of the gifts of the outdoors is that it comes with infinite loose parts such as rocks, sticks, leaves, and sand. Further, these natural materials are ambiguous and open to being shaped by the play of children into whatever it is that the children want to express. In contrast, manufactured toys often come with a story already embedded in them, a suggested meaning, and a message to children about how to use them and what to play. This restricts the imagination in a way that nature does not. Nature's loose parts are free educational materials. They are readily available, fascinating to children, and absorb their attention for extended periods of time.

In **Rock Man** on page 96, a handful of nothing but gravel and quartz becomes the vehicle for extended reasoning and problem solving.

In **Oak Apple Gall** on page 154, the children are inspired to observe closely and talk together about the green balls they have found. They reflect, apply, and interpret their experience over a period of several days, drawing, reading about, and telling others about their discovery.

The story **Frog House** on page 152, depicts an even more sophisticated application of reflection and interpretation. In it, Theo uses loose parts he has collected—both natural materials, such as moss, bark, and lichen, and a plastic frog—to represent and explore his expanding knowledge about frogs and frog behavior.

The Bakery on page 85 illustrates how the availability of diverse loose parts supports children's imagination and inventiveness and extends their play. Beginning with standard cake pans, measuring cups, and sand, the children assemble beautiful "cakes." They decorate them using colorful leaves, twigs, brown seeds, and acorns in their pretend play roles as bakers.

In each of these narratives, the availability of open-ended loose parts allows children to find just what they need to best express their ideas and explore their questions. You can see the importance of having a large number of diverse materials available in the environment so that children can engage with the particular ideas they are striving to understand.

The Role of Living Things

How animals and plants live, grow, and die is deeply interesting to both children and adults. The life cycle of plants as they move from seed to sprout to mature plant to seed dispersal follows a predictable sequence children can observe. They can also observe a tremendous variety of unique plant adaptations, comparing parts, shapes, and sizes, species to species. Children are eager to understand the activities of the plants around them and to recognize and learn the stages the plants go through. Children are also intently interested in the life cycle of animals. Animals follow the simple but ultimately predictable pattern of being born (or hatched), growing up, living, and then dying. Some patterns, such as for amphibians and insects, comprise a more complicated life cycle that includes the magic of metamorphosis. Insects provide children with a chance to observe complete metamorphosis as they move from egg to larva to pupa to adult. The stages and changes children can witness in the growth and development of both plants and animals are full of puzzles, mysteries, and things to observe, wonder about, and figure out. Outdoors, children can see these stages replicated again and again as part of their environment, each time in a slightly different and fascinating way.

Garden Day on page 70 illustrates the opportunities growing plants and creating gardens outdoors with children can provide. As revealed through the story, the activity involves children's entire bodies as they dig, place, and water the plants in a bed. By maintaining the garden throughout the growing season, children are able to observe the changes and stages of the plants they have planted. The adults around them carefully work to provide only the amount of help the children need to feel confident and independent. Hands-on experiences like these and the opportunity to take responsibility for the care of the plants enables children to feel a sense of ownership that eventually leads to stewardship.

Sweet Stevia on page 35 illustrates the deep and genuine relationships children develop with school gardens and with the individual plants in those gardens over time. Michael has learned so many things about the Stevia growing in his school's Taste Me garden; he knows its smell and taste, and the shape of its leaves. He applies the knowledge and expresses the connection he feels with this individual plant as he searches for the Stevia in the now much-changed winter garden.

In the story **The Dead Bird** on page 24, Jared's discovery of a dead bird in the parking lot inspires deep curiosity amongst his group. A lively discussion ensues in which the children articulate their questions and predictions about how and why the bird died, a conversation that is inexorably linked to their bigger questions about life and death.

In the story **The Millipede** on page 150, Shelby and Quinn are transfixed watching the activities of the multilegged insect. They notice in detail how it looks, moves, and behaves. They display the confidence and ease that children develop from repeated opportunities to observe, notice, and learn about animals outside. The girls take an active interest in what the millipede is doing, where it is going, and why it might be going there. They apply what they know about animals, reflect on what they see, and interpret what it might mean.

Observing and learning about plants and animals outside—their behavior, their needs, and their life cycles—prompt children to engage with the standards and with higher-level thinking. These experiences encourage children to apply varied learning approaches to different problems as they strive to answer questions they develop about what they see happening around them.

The Teacher's Role in Provisioning

Provisioning, in this context, refers to all of the loose parts and plant and animal life that the environment offers to children. Materials and interesting experiences abound in the natural world. It comes provisioned for learning. But provisioning also refers to the important role teachers have in providing and selecting appropriate materials and instruction outdoors. Both art and professional judgment are involved in knowing what materials may best support and extend children's learning at any point in time. Experience and judgment are required to know when, what kind, and how much instruction children need. Since the goal is for children to feel empowered and independent, careful consideration is needed in determining if and when to intercede. Provisioning includes scientific picture books and storybooks at different reading levels, magnifying lenses and drawing materials, costuming materials and music, and eventually materials for making a set for a child-written play. Each of these contributions is offered in response to the direction of the children's interest, sustaining and furthering their pursuit of ideas and questions over time. Below are stories that demonstrate how and when to provide concrete materials and objects to extend children's learning. They also describe the provision of instruction, a more abstract but essential application of this same idea.

In **Praying Mantis** on page 109, the teacher notices the children's growing interest in the insects in the garden. Over a period of a month, she provides successive material resources to support their interest in answering the questions generated through their exploration. Here, the materials are a means for the children to engage with the standard: discussing, consulting, and collaborating with other children and adults in working through questions and investigations (Reasoning and Problem Solving, indicator 4).

In **Clay Roses** on page 165, the roles of both materials and instructional provisioning are explored. The story shows how the two work together to support children's learning. The teacher has set out a comfortable work space and provided abundant clay and many types of tools for working with it. What is not mentioned directly in the story itself is the instruction that the teacher had previously provided. She had been giving impromptu mini-lessons all year long in response to each child's readiness and interest. These lessons included how to use the tools, how to cut a chunk of clay from the large slab, how to knead the clay to remove air bubbles so it doesn't explode in the kiln, how to join pieces of clay so they stay together. The children explored and practiced their skills over time. Molly was, in this story, able to take on the role of teacher because her learning was so solid and complete. Because of her teacher's careful provisioning of materials and instruction, Molly demonstrated a sense of optimism, ownership, and a realistic sense of personal control (Flexibility and Resilience, indicator 1).

Teacher provisioning relies on observing and reflecting. These are critical professional skills required in early childhood education. In the dynamic setting of the outdoors, children are constantly taking initiative, making discoveries, and planning many of their own activities. With such a range of possible actions and outcomes, teachers often witness children engaged in powerful learning activities that were not anticipated. Children are self-selecting and designing their own activities outdoors as they follow their own interests. This makes the outdoors a busier and less predictable environment than the inside. The unexpected and unplanned nature of children's learning outside makes the ability to observe, reflect, and interpret in the moment indispensable.

The Teacher's Role in Extending Learning

By watching and listening carefully, you can understand the important work children are doing outdoors and what it is they need from you. Do they need additional tools or materials to follow their idea? These might include drawing paper and markers to record their observations, a guidebook to look up an insect they have seen, a magnifying lens to look more closely at an interesting rock, or music and costumes to extend their play. Do they need an opportunity to have a conversation about what they are seeing or experiencing to clarify their thinking?

"Tell me about what you found."

"What do you think the bug uses this long part for?"

"Where do you think this little pod came from?"

Do they need a well-placed question that helps extend their thinking? "What do you think would happen if you tried a different block to hold up your bridge?"

Alternatively, what they may need is more time and space to work on their own without interruption or intervention. Understanding children's work and play outdoors and knowing how to respond often requires sophisticated judgment. Observation and reflection skills are refined as you spend time outside and practice them. Observing children and their activities will improve your ability to plan for their interests and needs and boost the quality of what you provide for them.

In **The Big Push** on page 134, Eliza appears to be involved in a task that is too much for her; despite many attempts, she is not able to push the big trike up the hill. Instead of intervening immediately, her teacher observes closely and long enough to realize that rather than becoming frustrated, Eliza is engaged with the challenge and is fine-tuning her approach. Eliza adjusts her strategy based on information she gains from each attempt she makes. By providing her with space and time to persist, this skilled teacher makes it possible for Eliza to succeed.

In **The Zipper** on page 29, Madison is involved with one of the most frustrating activities children face, learning to zip up a winter jacket. Many adults are tempted to tie children's shoes and zip their jackets for them rather than letting them work at it themselves. There are many reasons for this: saving time, avoiding frustration, and keeping zippers and laces from getting all tangled up! However, allowed to experiment and work at this intriguing challenge, Madison succeeds in learning how to zip up her own jacket. She does it independently, with confidence and pride. When she then offers to help a friend with her zipper, the teacher gives her time and support to apply her skill at this next most difficult level. Her teacher, by maintaining an easy-going attitude and being ready to intervene if needed, helps Madison consolidate her new skill.

These stories offer examples of teachers offering children opportunities to extend their own learning. In each case, the teacher looks for opportunities to provide children with the resources they need to do it themselves. There is a great benefit to children when teachers are patient and observe carefully, watching and waiting before jumping in.

The Role of Children's Relationship with Nature

Children's experiences outdoors allow them to witness how interrelated and interdependent everyone and everything really is. It is in the natural world that they find tangible proof that everything is connected with everything else. Here, they come to realize and internalize that they, as human beings, are an integral part of the world around them. A seamless outcome of their work and play outdoors is an emerging understanding of the rules that govern the natural world. Children are able to construct for themselves a mental model of how this complex physical system works. They pour water, and over a period of time, they learn that it always flows downhill. They plant seedlings and watch them stretch toward the sun. They observe trees shed their leaves in the fall and grow new ones in the spring. In addition to the ongoing cycles and systems they observe, they experience how they themselves affect the environment and how the environment affects them.

In **To Catch a Leaf** on page 175, Phin is involved in a game with the falling leaves in which he constantly adjusts his movements, trying to anticipate the speed and direction the leaves will take. The leaves themselves are responding to the change of season: shed by the tree, they are pulled by gravity and pushed by the force of the wind. This complex dance is an expression of the interconnectedness of all the players: tree, gravity, wind, weather, and child. By participating, Phin learns more about the fall world around him.

In **Snow Scale** on page 65, Kiri is able to develop and follow through on a plan because her investigation has revealed to her a rule about how snow responds to pressure. Her persistence is rewarded with the discovery of an underlying rule of nature. By applying pressure to the snow with her hands, and then a board, she compresses the snow, a process that releases heat and forms ice. Through trial and error, she creates the effect she is looking for and discovers how she can use the ice like glue to bind the boards together.

Water Works on page 42 shows what happens when children are able to spend a long time with a project or idea. Creating a project together, the children have many opportunities to observe the behavior of water. They observe and respond to the water's powerful movement downhill and its ability to move other objects before it. Damming and redirecting the water enables them to play with cause and effect, and to better understand the nature of the materials they are working with.

Playing in nature is endlessly fun and interesting. Children respond to its constant invitations to touch, test, explore, notice, and take a closer look. This is a process that reveals to them the underlying dependability of its structure. Being part of its rhythms and rules and privy to some of its secrets gives them a strong sense of belonging. Given time and opportunity, children form a deep relationship with the natural world in which they feel increasingly at home.

The Teacher's Role in Relationship Building

At the core of the work you do as a teacher are the relationships you build with children. It is the quality of these relationships that determines how appropriately and helpfully you can interact with each child. It affects how you respond to their growth, development, and needs. When you know the children well and develop trusting and affirming connections with them, you create the environment necessary to provide useful supports, beneficial interventions, and appropriate child-centered teaching.

Creating and developing dynamic, genuine, and vibrant relationships with children is demanding work. It requires many skills that are refined throughout the course of your professional life. These include strong interpersonal skills, a well-developed ability to communicate, perceptive and acute listening skills, and cultivated observation skills, as well as a clear, well-grounded professional understanding of early childhood development. Relationship building also requires an ongoing openness to learning. Through experience, training, and practice, you constantly gain new skills, refine tools and approaches, and add to your repertoire an understanding of how best to work with and on behalf of young children.

As this book demonstrates, much of children's learning outdoors grows out of the materials, changes, and "happenings" occurring around them. In this environment, most of the direct teaching you do comes straight from the content or the experience in front of you. Just like the children, you must become immersed and tuned in to the experiences at hand. You must be a learner "in the moment." By sharing your questions, discoveries, and wonder with children, you develop a partnership with them that engenders trust.

The hands-on nature of outdoor learning places great emphasis on relationships with children and requires the ability to be responsive to them and their needs in the moment. When children experience safe, trusting relationships, they are more communicative; ask more questions; share more of their observations; and feel more confident expressing their concerns, interests, and successes. Building strong relationships with children encourages dialogue and inquiry, essential components of young children's learning. Flexibility and understanding are essential teaching tools in early childhood settings, particularly in the outdoors, where children engage in so many open-ended projects.

In **The Bakery** on page 85, the teacher's caring relationship with a child assists her in understanding and providing for his needs and sensibilities. Liam has spent a great deal of time and effort baking his pretend cake. When cleanup time is suddenly announced, his teacher recognizes immediately the disappointment he feels at being asked to dump out his hard work. Her understanding of young children and her sensitivity to their feelings, paired with her ability to be flexible and think quickly on her feet, allows her to suggest a solution. Leaving his cake out for the birds meets Liam's needs while also meeting the school's need to bring outdoor time to closure with cleanup.

The story **Squirrel Cache** on page 53 shows what happens when teachers forget to trust children to make valuable discoveries. It also provides a useful example of how direct teaching can sometimes impede important discovery learning. William is deeply engaged in finding signs of winter animal activity as his school group walks through the woods. He is focused and alert as he scans the ground for interesting things to investigate. He spots a most unusual find, an actual squirrel cache where the animal has stored food for the winter. The teachers leading his group, however, are not focused on the children but rather are focused on finding signs of winter that they can show the children. Because the teachers are looking for content they can teach, rather than letting the children interact with the environment, William's discovery almost goes unnoticed.

Teachers who develop strong, positive relationships with children learn that they can trust children to be natural, motivated, curious learners. These teachers are more skilled at engaging with and extending children's own discovery learning.

The Umbrella Project Approach

Activities and projects outdoors often have a structure that comes from the natural environment. Outdoors, everything is connected to everything else. Butterflies appear when flowers bloom. Birds arrive as berries ripen. Dust kicks up when the ground dries out. Mud appears when it rains. Teachers can learn to understand and use this quality of interconnectedness to provide powerful learning experiences for children. Outdoors children experience firsthand the cause and effect of natural occurrences as well as the predictable sequence of plant and animal life.

The result of the interconnected content in the outdoors is that every planned activity contains within it many additional activities and investigations fascinating to children. If teachers are open to letting children engage with the content of an activity in the numerous ways their interests lead them, new activities and investigations will unfold naturally. This open-ended approach to planning involves designing a compelling project and providing materials for exploring it in a number of different ways. This approach is referred to in the following examples as the "umbrella project approach."

Potato Story on page 55 shows how perfectly "umbrella projects" unfold in the out-of-doors. Here, a discrete activity planned by the teacher, planting potatoes in the garden, spawns myriad investigations and inspires children's independent activities. The potato planting serves as an umbrella under which distinct and separate smaller projects emerge. While some children engage in a straightforward way with the planting itself, others branch off. Some find worms in the soil as they dig and observe and want to talk about what the worms are doing. Others uncover an old potato from last year and wonder if it is a stone. They devise an experiment to find out. Several more explore the remnants of a rotting pumpkin. Two children interested in making a sign to label the potato garden bring reading and writing under the project's umbrella.

The Teacher's Role in the Umbrella Approach

All of this varied content emerges naturally as children engage at different levels. The broad range of ideas seen in the Potato Story example is deeper and more complex than their teacher could have explicitly planned for. For many teachers, this is a new and different way of teaching. It is less scripted and less predictable than a traditional lesson plan but it is not unstructured. It has a multifaceted structure embedded in the ideas and the content itself. It is this structure that enables teachers to partner with children to find just the right learning activity for each child to be fully engaged and successful. This method of teaching is a very efficient way to individualize instruction and to challenge children appropriately. Teaching this way is fun, busy, and challenging. It encourages children's autonomy and it is more satisfying for teachers than trying to lead every child through the same planned lesson.

How do teachers plan for and structure a successful umbrella project? Start by observing and listening to children as they work and play outdoors. Projects emerge from children's interests. Look for what children gravitate toward and want to learn more about. Projects are often inspired by changes in the weather and the seasons, by naturally occurring events, and by ideas that emerge from children's own experiences. Think beyond the classroom to children's experiences at home and in the community as well as with each other. Look to books and other materials that captivate children. Be on the lookout for big ideas that can be explored through the design of a meaningful project.

Garden Day on page 70 captures a day in the life of an umbrella project that, like Potato Story, involves planting. The children are involved in planting a school garden. They have been provided with the tools to dig, plant, and water some new spring plants. From the planned planting activity described in the story, other activities emerge. Some children decide to investigate the small orchard near the garden. They discover tent caterpillars in the shadbush trees. Several girls don beautiful gowns from the costume bin and pretend to be fairies, watering the blueberry bushes. Another child arranges and rearranges a planting of artificial flowers, exploring color patterns and shapes. Two children arrange all the garden gloves in matching pairs. They practice putting the gloves on and taking them off again. Another child spends most of the garden time not planting, but digging and filling holes by himself. Their teacher, by structuring and provisioning the environment around the big idea of gardening and growing plants, enables the children to initiate activities following one of the many threads included in this big idea.

Planning as an Ongoing Process

Umbrella projects shelter an enormous range of activities, explorations, and ideas. They offer a group of children a way of sharing and learning from each other in the midst of their differences in interest, ability, and level of skill. They offer teachers the opportunity to engage with children who are highly motivated, connecting with content at a level that is challenging and rewarding for them. Umbrella projects are open ended. Rather than presenting children with a task to do, they offer them a menu of ideas, increasing the chances that each will find that "just right fit."

In Potato Story, The Bridge, and Praying Mantis, the umbrella projects the teacher designed were both broad and deep. Each project encompassed a diverse and compelling range of smaller projects. Such diversity ensures that all children can and will participate. These stories illustrate that planning is a process, not a static structure. The plan is a place to start, not a final destination or product. Teachers plan an activity, providing materials and tools. They then observe how children engage and respond to what has been provided.

You cannot know initially just how the children's interests, questions, and abilities may sculpt the designed plan. By watching, listening, and reflecting, teachers learn what fine-tuning and adjustments to make to support the directions children begin to take. This kind of ongoing restructuring is a necessary partner to planning. For example, an activity may turn out to be too complex and need to be broken down into smaller, more manageable parts. It may take longer than anticipated and need to be spread out over many days. Perhaps the children need more information, different materials, or a different approach in order to engage with growing independence. Sometimes children need assistance for a portion of the project so that they can participate and understand the whole.

In **Garden Day** on page 70, Keisha wants to learn how to garden but she is not ready to do it by herself. Keisha's mom is able to see exactly how much and what kind of help to provide so that Keisha can complete as much of the planting as she is ready to do on her own. By restructuring the task and providing just the right amount of help, Keisha's mom adjusts the fit between Keisha's level of skill and the task that Keisha wants to accomplish. Participating successfully in this way, Keisha gains confidence and a better understanding of the big picture, which she can apply with more independence in the future.

Restructuring of the kind described here is often challenging on many levels. It requires that teachers be alert and responsive and be able to think outside the box. It may involve abandoning one plan or direction in order to follow the lead of the children. The greatest support for teachers when restructuring is a rich environment that offers children the materials, tools, and loose parts they need to pursue the new directions their discoveries and questions may take.

The Role of Change in Outdoor Learning

Teaching outside requires being able to adapt to unexpected events. These may take a variety of forms. A change in the weather, the sudden appearance or disappearance of a spider web, the leaves turning red, a puddle drying up— all are changes that capture children's interest in a predictable and powerful way. They draw children to investigate and wonder what happened and what it might mean. Outdoors, the weather, the temperature, the light, and the behavior and appearance of plants and animals all change and vary season to season, day to day, hour to hour, even minute to minute. This constant change is engaging and exciting to children, and invites them to notice and ask "why?" The stories recounted in this book show how change calls to children, sparking their curiosity and imagination. Change creates learning opportunities that engage children with all of the early learning standards.

In **The Mystery of the Vine** on page 33, Adrian is drawn by the difference between what he expects to find when he holds the vine and what he actually experiences. This discrepancy is motivating and invites him to wonder about what is going on, and to investigate and discover the cause of the change.

In **Cloud Study** on page 179, something as ever-present as the movement of clouds captivates children's attention. Watching the movement of clouds is an endlessly fascinating activity, involving children in speculation and open-ended questioning. They ask, "What makes them move?" "What makes them change shape?" "Where do they go?"

In **Pussy Willow** on page 146, Sage notices the vivid changes in the catkins on the pussy willow tree, comparing them to each other and making predictions about what will happen next.

In **The Carrot** on page 98, as tiny a prompt as a different-shaped leaf in the ground ivy bed catches the notice of the children. It prompts them to investigate further until they discover remnants of last year's carrots.

Change is an important starting point for children's questions. The more opportunities children have to notice, experience, and investigate changes in their environment, the more involved they become with the early learning standards.

Conclusion

A common thread weaves through all of the stories in this book. It is the powerful conversation or dialogue between children, their environment, and their teachers in rich outdoor settings. This three-way conversation is at the heart of outdoor learning. Each of the participants brings a strong individual voice to this dialogue. Teachers, children, and the environment all work together outdoors in a powerful partnership to support children's engagement with the early learning standards. Children come curious and ready to learn. To do this, they need a truly diverse environment with which to interact. Children also need the partnership of engaged, observant teachers who care about and are planning for learning in that environment. To engage with the standards, all three players are needed: the curious child, the involved teacher, and the diverse natural environment.

The experiences and activities documented here represent profound and challenging education. Once the traditional and restrictive assumptions about the outdoors are put aside, teachers can enter the outdoors and use it as the key support to early learning standards and approaches to learning. Observing firsthand and analyzing what children are actually doing outside helps this process. Thinking about and reflecting on these stories provides a new lens for you to understand how valuable and critical the outdoors is as a site for learning. Using the models in this book gives you a chance to practice looking more closely, to interpret more accurately, and think more deeply about the process unfolding in children's play outdoors. As Rachel Carson, nature writer and environmentalist, observed years ago, "If a child is to keep alive his inborn sense of wonder without any such gift from the fairies, he needs the companionship of at least one adult who can share it, rediscovering with him the joy, excitement and mystery of the world we live in" (1956). We all have an opportunity to be that adult.

APPENDIX

Standards and Indicators for Three- to Five-Year-Olds by Chapter

Curiosity and Initiative Standard, Chapter 2

1. The child demonstrates eagerness to learn by asking questions, developing ideas, and exploring objects and materials. (page 22)
2. The child expresses interest in others and initiates interactions. (page 27)
3. The child wonders about the world and is open to new experiences. (page 31)
4. The child uses a variety of senses to explore the world and experience answers to questions. (page 35)
5. The child invents projects and works on them with growing independence. (page 39)

Engagement and Persistence Standard, Chapter 3

1. The child concentrates on a variety of age-appropriate tasks, activities, and projects despite distractions or interruptions. (page 50)
2. The child pursues increasingly complex tasks, projects, and activities, willingly working on them over a period of hours or days. (page 55)
3. The child continues to attempt a difficult task, sustaining attention and working through attendant frustration, disappointment, difficulties, and obstacles. (page 61)
4. The child purposefully chooses activities and interactions of interest, develops a plan, and follows through with increasing independence. (page 65)
5. The child seeks and accepts help, information, tools, and materials from peers and adults when needed. (page 70)

Imagination, Invention, and Creativity Standard, Chapter 4

1. The child exhibits, appreciates, and enjoys a sense of humor. (page 78)
2. The child engages in pretend play, expressing feelings, trying out new ideas and behaviors, and role playing using real or make-believe objects. (page 82)
3. The child explores and experiments, trying new ways of doing things by combining and using materials in novel and original ways. (page 87)

Reasoning and Problem-Solving Standard, Chapter 5

1. The child actively explores the environment and identifies meaningful issues. (page 96)
2. The child initiates more than one approach or solution in response to questions and dilemmas. (page 100)
3. The child applies strategies such as trial and error, comparing, sorting, classifying, and organizing to understand and find solutions. (page 104)
4. The child discusses, consults, and collaborates with other children and adults in working through questions and investigations. (page 109)

Risk-Taking, Responsibility, and Confidence Standard, Chapter 6

1. The child chooses appropriate physical, social, and cognitive challenges, demonstrating growing awareness of his or her own ability. (page 121)
2. The child sets goals and follows through on plans with increasing independence. (page 125)
3. The child communicates his or her own ideas and opinions in interactions with others—both peers and adults. (page 130)
4. The child expresses delight and satisfaction when solving problems or completing tasks. (page 134)

Reflection, Interpretation, and Application Standard, Chapter 7

1. The child relates past experience to new situations, generating ideas, increasing understanding, and making predictions. (page 144)
2. The child speculates and demonstrates a beginning understanding of motivations and intentions, and what others are thinking. (page 148)
3. The child uses play, representation, and discussion to process information and apply ideas. (page 152)

Flexibility and Resilience Standard, Chapter 8

1. The child demonstrates a sense of optimism, ownership, and a realistic sense of personal control. (page 163)

2. The child is willing to attempt tasks that previously were difficult. (page 168)

3. The child shows a growing ability to control impulses, accepting and adjusting to unplanned, unwanted, and unexpected events or outcomes. (page 173)

4. The child demonstrates comfort with open-ended questions and problems. (page 178)

References

Carson, Rachel. 1956. *The sense of wonder.* New York: HarperCollins.

Gill, Tim. 2007. *No fear, growing up in a risk averse society.* London: Calouste Gulbenkin Foundation.

Kagan, Jerome. 2002. *Surprise, uncertainty, and mental structures.* Cambridge, MA: Harvard University Press.

Montaigne, Michel. 1580. *Essais.* Quoted in *The Oxford dictionary of quotations* (Oxford: Oxford University Press, 2004), 544.

Moore, Robin C. and Herb H. Wong. 1997. *Natural learning: Creating environments for rediscovering nature's way of teaching.* Berkeley: MIG Communications.

Muir, John. 1911. *My first summer in the Sierra.* Boston: Houghton Mifflin Company.

Nicholson, Simon. 1971. How not to cheat children: The theory of loose parts. *Landscape Architecture* 62: 30–35.

Paley, Vivian Gussin. 1988. *Bad guys don't have birthdays: Fantasy play at four.* Chicago and London: The University of Chicago Press.

Pellegrini, Anthony D. 1995. *School recess and playground behavior: Educational and developmental roles.* Albany: State University of New York Press.

Rogers, Fred. 1983. *Mr. Rogers talks with parents.* New York: Berkley Books.

Rousseau, Jean-Jacques. 2003. *Emile or treatise on education.* Amherst, NY: Prometheus Books.

St. Giermaine, Joyce. 1994. Out of the classroom . . . into the garden. Speech presented at the International Symposium on the Prepared Learning Environment, Arlington, VA. Quoted in M. Rivkin, *The great outdoors: Restoring children's right to play outside* (Washington, DC: NAEYC, 1995), 8.

Taylor, Faber, F. E. Kuo, and W. C. Sullivan. 2001. Coping with ADD: The surprising connection to green place settings. *Environment and Behavior* 33, no. 1: 54–77.

Tough, Paul. 2009. Can the right kinds of play teach self-control? *New York Times Magazine: The School Issue*. September 27.

Vandenberg, B. 1986. Play theory. In G. Fein, *The young child at play: Reviews of research,* ed. M. Rivkin, 17–22. Washington, DC: NAEYC.

Wood, Chip. 1997. *Yardsticks: Children in the classroom ages 4–14, a resource for parents and teachers.* Turners Falls, MA: Northeast Foundation for Children.

Photography Credits

Photographs on the following pages are by Wendy Banning: xii, 6, 18, 23, 24, 25, 27, 31, 35, 38, 39, 40, 42, 43, 44, 51, 55, 56, 58, 59, 61, 64, 66, 68, 70, 74, 80, 82, 83, 85, 87, 90, 92, 96, 97, 99, 100, 101, 104, 105, 107, 109, 114, 125, 130, 132, 134, 135, 137, 140, 144, 148, 150, 152, 154, 155, 158, 165, 166, 168, 171, 173, 175, 176, and 182.

Photographs on the following pages are by Ginny Sullivan: 29, 33, 37, 41, 42, 46, 53, 62, 64, 72, 78, 85, 89, 103, 109, 111, 121, 123, 127, 128, 146, 163, 168, 169, 178, and 180.